SEX
ED

SEX ED

DR. MIRIAM STOPPARD

Illustrated by
Sally Artz

DK PUBLISHING, INC.

*To the pupils of
Caldicott School, for whom I have
the deepest respect*

A DK PUBLISHING BOOK

MANAGING EDITOR Jemima Dunne
MANAGING ART EDITOR Lynne Brown

PROJECT EDITOR Nicky Adamson
EDITOR Debbie Voller
EDITORIAL ASSISTANT Fergus Collins
US EDITOR Laaren Brown

SENIOR ART EDITOR Karen Ward
ART EDITOR Luke Herriott
DESIGNER Chloë Steers

PRODUCTION CONTROLLER
Manjit Sihra

First American Edition, 1997
2 4 6 8 10 9 7 5 3 1
Published in the United States by
DK Publishing, Inc.
95 Madison Avenue, New York, New York 10016

Visit us on the World Wide Web at
http://www.dk.com

Library of Congress Cataloging-in-Publication Data
Stoppard, Miriam / Sex ed / p. cm. / Includes index.
Summary: A guide to growing up, relationships, and sex,
discussing such topics as male and female anatomy, petting,
intercourse, different kinds of sexual activities, contraception,
and safe sex. ISBN 0-7894-2385-5 hc 0-7894-1751-0 paper
1. Sex instruction for teenagers. 2. Man-woman
relationships–Juvenile literature. 3. Hygiene, Sexual-Juvenile
literature. (1. Sex instruction for youth.) I. Title
HQ35.S876   1998 97–14341
613.9′51—dc21   CIP AC

Reproduced by Colourscan, Singapore
Printed in Italy by New Interlitho S.P.A., Milan

CONTENTS

INTRODUCTION

"You've got my respect!"

I HAVE WRITTEN THIS BOOK out of respect for teenagers. When you respect people, you defend their rights, you consider their needs, you want to help resolve their difficulties, you are sensitive to their feelings, and you are concerned about how they grow and develop. For me, as a mother, a doctor, and a writer, my respect goes one step further: I want you to have good information that helps you make sound choices as you struggle toward sexual maturity.

YOU NEED INFORMATION

No one can persuade me that children and teenagers should be deprived of information about sex. If children become familiar with the basics of sexuality as a normal part of growing up, at a level that causes them no discomfort, so much the better. Detractors can no longer claim that sex education encourages permissiveness; in fact it does the reverse, and there is much research to support this. There are few other ways of encouraging responsible, caring, loving sexual behavior than through good sex education.

CONSIDERATION FOR OTHERS

One of my goals is to make you think and reflect. In the area of sexuality, I would like to encourage you to think about the consequences of your actions before they happen – and to examine your own feelings. What makes you feel comfortable? What do you consider wrong? At what point would you say "no"? What would make you feel really upset, taken advantage of, ashamed or guilty – and would you have the courage to say so? Would you be brave enough to speak up and defend others as well as yourself? Sometimes it can be very difficult to resist pressures, whether you are a girl who's scared a boy will dump you if you don't have sex, or a

"The best advice is to be true to yourself."

"I do love you, but I want us to take things slowly."

boy who feels that you have to lose your virginity to keep up with your friends. Of course you want to feel you "belong," everyone does, but the pain of not being true to yourself is infinitely greater than the initial discomfort of resisting peer pressure. You will discover that the latter lasts only for a few months, while the former can last a lifetime.

RIGHTS AND RESPONSIBILITIES

Besides the right to full and frank information on sexual matters, I believe you should always be taken seriously; you have the right to fair and open discussion, to express opinions, and then to make your own choices and decisions. With rights come responsibilities, and by fulfilling them you can raise your self-esteem and express your maturity. Remember, your sexual responsibilities to others are just as important as those toward yourself. One of the best yardsticks you can apply to any challenging situation is this golden rule: Ask yourself, "How would I like to be treated?" And then, whatever you decide, make sure that you treat others in the same way.

"It's your turn to decide where we go tonight!"

IS THERE A RIGHT AGE FOR SEX?

I'm often asked, "What is the right age to start having sex?" But a better question would be, "What would make me unready for sex?" Please take a look at the questions on page 14, and if the answer is "yes" to any of them, you're *definitely* not ready. Sex should always be seen as an expression of love and is never something to be entered into lightly. Indeed it is against the law until you reach your late teens. But with the help of this book, I hope you'll have the information to enable you make sensible decisions about sex, both now and later in life.

THINGS FIRST

Maturity, and Responsibility

As your sexual awareness increases, it's easy to lose sight of simple friendship. Friendships are more precious than any other kind of relationship; they bring out the best in you because you learn to consider the needs of other people, so they have to be the basis of a loving sexual relationship. How you behave with friends and family reflects how mature you are. Maturity goes hand-in-hand with the ability to develop a responsible attitude toward your sexual relationships.

I don't think I could ever be like those girls. I guess I should just be myself.

...he makes the basket. The crowd has gone wild! They love him!

MAKING FRIENDS

Friends become more **IMPORTANT** in your *teens*

Friends help you *broaden* your **INTERESTS**

Friends give one other **LOYALTY** and *support*

WHY FRIENDS ARE IMPORTANT

The desire to have friends goes very deep – children start to make friends outside their own family starting as young as two years old. But for young children, family and home are by far the most important. Now that you're a teenager, you probably feel that your home life and family don't give you enough. You want to broaden your interests, you need people with different backgrounds, you want to try out new activities and belong to a group where everyone thinks and dresses alike, and shares common values.

Friends of your own age matter a lot, and you want to spend as much time as possible with them. You may begin to feel there's a growing rift between you and your parents and that they often cannot see your point of view. You turn to your friends instead – they know what you're experiencing, they're sympathetic with your views, and they make you feel that you belong.

THREE'S COMPANY

"Hey, guess what! That great guy Gary's asked me out. I'm seeing him Friday."

"Oh, I thought we were going to a movie. Still, I suppose Gary's more important."

REMEMBER...A good friendship . . . .

WHAT'S A FRIEND?

- Someone who likes you.
- Someone you care about.
- Someone to confide in.
- Someone to share with.
- Someone you can rely on.
- Someone who likes the same things as you.
- Someone to give advice.
- Someone who will always stick up for you.
- Someone who balances your weaknesses.
- Someone who values your help.
- Someone to share jokes with.
- Someone who will always tell you the truth.
- Someone who believes in you.
- Someone who'll tell you straight that you're wrong.
- Someone who worries about you.
- Someone who doesn't get jealous.
- Someone you support.
- Someone who makes you feel good about yourself.
- Someone whose opinion you really value.
- Someone who'll keep a secret.
- Someone who introduces you to new things.

WHAT FRIENDS MEAN TO GIRLS

Going SHOPPING.

STICKING together.

Asking ADVICE.

Most girls value the close companionship of a tight-knit group. If one of the group starts dating, this upsets the balance. Try not to feel rejected when this happens. Your friend still needs you.

Turn the page to find out what friends mean to boys.

NEXT TIME . . .

Making friends doesn't come easily to everyone. Feeling like an outsider is depressing. Turn the page to find out how to make friends of both sexes.

"Why don't we go to a movie on Saturday – it's a better night anyway!"

I was silly to feel so jealous; we're still friends.

"He's gorgeous. I'm really happy for you. Has he got any nice friends?"

. . . is one where you both feel EQUAL.

MAKING FRIENDS *continued*

HOW TO MAKE FRIENDS

Straightforward friendships with other people of your own age are just as important as those that involve sexual attraction. In fact a relationship that isn't also a friendship won't work. But making friends is difficult for a lot of people. Joining a club or group is a great way to meet friends, but you may find that you haven't got the self-confidence to take the first steps. It helps to know that others are having the same problems.

TAKING THOSE FIRST STEPS

● Don't judge people too hastily; appearances can be deceptive.
● Be yourself rather than trying to imitate others or be top dog.
● Ask others about their interests, such as music or sports.
● Compliment someone on doing something well.

IF YOUR FRIENDS START DATING

Many young people worry about maintaining friendships as people start to pair off. One of your best friends may start being attracted to boys or girls when you're not interested yet. Another may find a partner, and you may feel jealous.

In the first instance, look around for someone who's in the same frame of mind as you and make a new friend. In the second, get a grip on your jealousy. Just because your friend has formed a new and close relationship doesn't mean he or she no longer values your friendship (see "Three's Company" on the previous page). If you start a relationship and your friend is jealous of you – be sympathetic.

If you're attracted to someone, keep your relationship at the level of friendship for as long as you can. The best way to earn someone's love is to be a friend.

SHARING INTERESTS

"Hey, James, I didn't know you could play like that."

"Have you ever heard this group? The keyboard player's excellent."

REMEMBER... Don't FAKE. Don't try...

GETTING HELP. . .

● Ask your parents what it was like when their best friends started going out with girls or boys. Parents can remember the pain very well and will be only too pleased to share their experiences.

● Your older brother or sister may tease you, but a sibling can give you good advice about flagging friendships, because they've been through the ups and downs.

● Talk to a mutual friend at school whose opinion you value and who knows everyone involved.

● Many books for young people deal realistically with problems about friendship. Ask at your local library for recommendations.

● You may find yourself under pressure from friends to behave in a way that you're unhappy with, simply because you want to remain part of a group (peer pressure). Talk to someone in your family about how you can stick to your guns.

● When you're up against peer pressure, learn how to say "no" and mean it (see page 50–1).

WHAT FRIENDS MEAN TO BOYS

Sports BUDDIES.

PROVIDING support.

Asking ADVICE.

Because teenage boys often develop a wide range of friends from different interest groups, going out with a girl doesn't interfere with their relationships with other boys.

See page 11 to find out what friends mean to girls.

NEXT TIME . . .
Friendship means giving and taking. Concentrate on your contribution to a friendship, not what it gives you, and you'll get more out of it.

"I know this great CD shop down on Market Street. Want to meet there?"

"Great store. And listen, I'm serious about forming a band. Let's go for it!"

. . . to be something you're not.

BECOMING MATURE

Being mature means you know **RIGHT** from *wrong*

Stand your *ground* and **RESIST** temptation

Act responsibly and **THINK** about other *people*

It's easy to see that you're maturing physically (see pages 20–3), but being emotionally mature is a different matter. People mature at different rates – but one thing's for sure: You shouldn't even think about having sex if you don't have a mature attitude about it.

MATURITY AND SEX

Young people often ask, "Am I old enough for sex?" There's no easy answer to this; everyone's different. Few people are mature enough to handle the worries and consequences of sex before their late teens, which is why in many countries it's actually against the law to have sex until you've reached your late teens.

"No, I can't come over. I said I'd help mom and dad clean the kitchen."

AM I MATURE?

- Would I stand up for a friend?
- Do I keep promises?
- Do I ask for advice?
- Can my parents trust me?
- Do I give, as well as take?
- Can I accept criticism?
- Can I postpone a treat?
- Do I give credit where it's due?

If you answered "no" to any of the above, you're not mature yet.

AM I READY FOR SEX?

- Do I think love is the same as infatuation?
- Would I have sex with someone I didn't love?
- Would I have a one-night stand?
- Would I insist on having sex?

If you answered "yes" to any of the above, you're not mature enough for a sexual relationship.

"Okay, I'm sorry. You're right, we don't know each other well enough yet."

REMEMBER... "I don't have to THINK...

GETTING HELP. . .

Talk to your parents

Most parents want to be asked for advice on all kinds of problems, so try to talk things through with them; being prepared to confide in your parents is a sign of maturity.

Relatives or friends

If it's difficult to ask questions about sex and emotional maturity at home, try other relatives such as your grandparents, or an older brother or sister, or perhaps a cousin. Or try friends – but make sure they are more mature and have some experience with the kind of difficulty you need help with.

Outside help

A teacher to whom you can talk frankly would be happy to help with problems about maturity, or perhaps a guidance counselor from your local school. If your problems have to do with health or sexuality, or if you are feeling depressed, then make an appointment to see your doctor. Turn to page 92 for some useful addresses and hotlines.

HOW TO BECOME MORE MATURE

Be a PEACEMAKER.

Give PRAISE.

Be TOLERANT.

PLAN ahead.

KEEP your promises.

Control your TEMPER.

ACCEPT good advice.

ADMIT you're wrong.

Act RESPONSIBLY.

"No, thanks. Not my style."

"Look, Dad... Ben... why don't we sit down and talk about this?"

NEXT TIME . . .

Think about:

- What the consequences of your actions might be.
- Other people's feelings before your own.
- How you'd like to be treated, and act accordingly.
- Being more self-disciplined.

. . . about 'ME' all the time."

ACTING RESPONSIBLY

Being responsible means you're *accountable* to **OTHERS**

It's **SENSIBLE** to approach *relationships* responsibly

Irresponsibility leads to **TROUBLE** in the long run

That does it, I'm in big trouble now!

WORRIES AND QUESTIONS. . .

Rebellion is a normal part of dealing with the emotional changes of adolescence. You may feel rebellious about the rules and regulations that society tries to impose on you, or, closer to home, those that your parents expect you to live by. Rather than taking your anger out on others, try saying "I'd like to be alone right now," and then leave the room. While every teenager has negative feelings, not all of them have blowups with their parents. Try to settle down and be a team member at home. It's better than being a loner.

WHAT IT MEANS TO BE RESPONSIBLE

As you grow older and you start thinking about having deeper relationships (which may involve sex eventually), you have to start paying attention to all of your responsibilities. Not just to your girl- or boyfriends, but to your family, your friends, and yourself.

Responsibility involves morality, which doesn't mean you have to be a real prude, it means having a clear idea of the boundaries of fairness and kindness in your behavior to others. You'll know when you're acting irresponsibly, because the consequences are hard to live with. And when you feel shame and guilt, your emotions create more unhappiness, because you're bound to take it out on others. Try to be true to yourself. People will respect you for it.

THINKING ABOUT OTHERS

Late again.... Dad's gonna go absolutely nuts as usual!

"*Dad, I missed the bus and I'm going to be a little late getting home. Sorry!*"

GUIDELINES FOR RESPONSIBLE SEX

Think before you leap into bed!

Girls

- No sex unless you really care about him, and he cares about you.
- No sex without some reliable form of birth control (see pages 62–3).
- Think about about how you'd cope if you got pregnant or contracted an STD.
- Think about how you'd feel the morning after a one-night stand.
- Learn how to say "no" and mean it (see page 51).

Boys

- No sex unless you really care about her, and she cares for you.
- Remember that pregnancy takes two – you're not a man if you won't share responsibility.
- Prevent STDs; always make sure that you wear a condom.
- Don't fake conquests and boast about girls you've never really had sex with.
- Think about how you'd feel the morning after a one-night stand.

WINNING YOUR PARENTS' TRUST

Parents usually give their children more freedom as they learn to trust them (see below); when they can talk to you without everything becoming an argument. With your parents on your side, you should feel safer and stronger than ever. Should your relationship with your parents ever break down really badly, there are people who can help. Turn to page 92 for some useful addresses and hotlines.

NEXT TIME . . .

Think about: If you've hurt someone, what could you do to avoid it in the future? Think before you act, and always try to imagine how the other person will feel.

"Late again! Oh, well... at least you managed to pick up the phone this time."

"Missing the bus gave me time to pick up that part you wanted for the car."

. . . responsible, you earn respect.

ING BODY

● ●

to Adulthood

As you mature physically and go through the changes of puberty, you may feel as if your body is playing tricks on you all the time. You'll even lose control of your moods; you'll be up on cloud nine one minute, and down in the dumps the next. But don't worry, you're not alone. All teenagers go through these highs and lows; you can blame it on your hormones. Things will settle down after a few years, as you move toward the inevitable climax of adulthood!

If you haven't got it, don't flaunt it! So I won't.

There's that girl again — and she's looking totally gorgeous. I'm glad I can cool off in the water.

HOW GIRLS WORK

Understanding your **BODY** helps you act *responsibly*

LEARN about the action of *hormones*

See also "How Boys Work," page 24

Girls go through great changes at puberty, but although their breasts are visibly growing, girls aren't aware of changes to their reproductive organs until their periods start (see page 22).

BREAST DEVELOPMENT

● Breasts come in every shape and size. Remember that it's not true that boys prefer girls with big breasts or that small breasts mean you can't feed a baby.

● It's normal for your breasts to feel tender as they grow during puberty, and in the week before your period. You may find that wearing a bra helps to relieve tenderness. A good support bra will keep heavy breasts in shape and stop them from bouncing.

WORRIES AND QUESTIONS. . .

Many girls worry about how their bodies look and feel, and find their growing sexual awareness disturbing. The "supermodels" used in fashion magazines promote an unrealistic, so-called ideal image of how girls should look, and it can be hard if you think that you don't match this ideal. A lot of girls (and increasingly boys) blame the way they look for their low self-esteem, which in turn may lead to more serious problems. If you feel bad about yourself, have the courage to ask for help before things get worse (see page 92 for useful addresses and hotlines).

GETTING HELP. . .

● Your mother is the best person for advice but if you can't talk to her, ask another older female relation who is sympathetic.

● Talk to a health teacher, school nurse, or guidance counselor, or see your doctor, and read as many books as you can.

● Compare notes with your best friend. Nearly everyone wonders if other girls are like them, and the answer is a reassuring yes. Most girls experience the same anxieties.

REMEMBER... Every young girl . . . .

HOW YOUR BODY CHANGES

Girls' bodies start to mature at about 10 years, and periods usually begin when girls are about 12, although anything between 10 and 16 years is normal (see page 22).

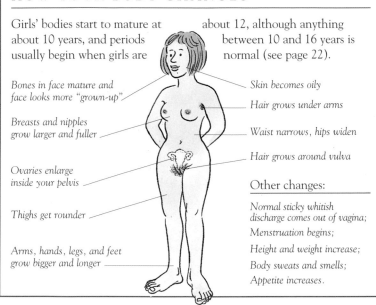

Bones in face mature and face looks more "grown-up".

Breasts and nipples grow larger and fuller

Ovaries enlarge inside your pelvis

Thighs get rounder

Arms, hands, legs, and feet grow bigger and longer

Skin becomes oily

Hair grows under arms

Waist narrows, hips widen

Hair grows around vulva

Other changes:

Normal sticky whitish discharge comes out of vagina;

Menstruation begins;

Height and weight increase;

Body sweats and smells;

Appetite increases.

WHAT HAPPENS INSIDE

Your reproductive organs fit snugly inside your pelvis, protected all around by your hip bones. The uterus (womb) measures about 3in (8cm), and each ovary is about 1.5in (3.5cm) long.

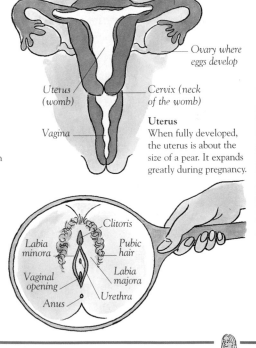

Fallopian tube

Ovary where eggs develop

Cervix (neck of the womb)

Uterus (womb)

Vagina

Vagina
About 4in (10cm) long from opening to cervix, the vagina is made of very elastic tissue so it can expand and extend during sexual intercourse and childbirth.

Uterus
When fully developed, the uterus is about the size of a pear. It expands greatly during pregnancy.

Your external anatomy
Familiarize yourself with your external anatomy by holding a mirror between your legs. The illustration here will help you identify what you can see.

Clitoris

Labia minora

Pubic hair

Labia majora

Vaginal opening

Urethra

Anus

. . experiences the same changes as you.

HOW GIRLS WORK *continued*

When you're around 12 years old, hormones from a gland in the brain (the pituitary gland) tell the ovaries to manufacture the female sex hormones, estrogen and progesterone. The ovaries start producing an egg every month, and you will begin to menstruate (to have periods). Although 12 is the average age for periods to begin, anything between 10 and 16 is normal. The start of menstruation is called menarche. Even before your first period you may be

fertile, which means that you can get pregnant if you have unprotected sex. Menstruation ends at menopause, when you're about 50.

THE MENSTRUAL CYCLE

Calculated from the first day of bleeding, the cycle is about 28 days. Hormones make the ovaries produce an egg, and the lining of the uterus grows. The egg travels to the uterus through the Fallopian tubes. If the egg isn't fertilized, it is shed with the uterus lining.

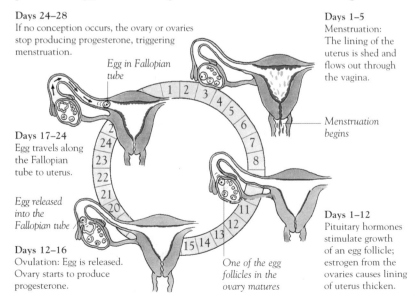

Days 24–28
If no conception occurs, the ovary or ovaries stop producing progesterone, triggering menstruation.

Egg in Fallopian tube

Days 1–5
Menstruation: The lining of the uterus is shed and flows out through the vagina.

Menstruation begins

Days 17–24
Egg travels along the Fallopian tube to uterus.

Egg released into the Fallopian tube

Days 12–16
Ovulation: Egg is released. Ovary starts to produce progesterone.

One of the egg follicles in the ovary matures

Days 1–12
Pituitary hormones stimulate growth of an egg follicle; estrogen from the ovaries causes lining of uterus thicken.

REMEMBER...Having periods is a kind of .

COPING WITH PERIODS

Your choice of pads and tampons

Ordinary napkin Bulky pad that fits inside pants usually with self-stick panel.	**Napkin with wings** Self-stick "wings" anchor the pad more securely inside pants.
Looped napkin with belt Sometimes more secure for heavy bleeding. The napkin is held in place between the legs by hooks on the belt. *Elastic belt*	**Panty liner** For light bleeding. Has adhesive panel.
	Tampon Small, convenient, but requires manual insertion.
Shaped napkin Fits inside pants. Held in place by adhesive panel.	**Tampon with applicator** Applicator pushes tampon into vagina.

How pads and tampons work

Sanitary napkin Worn externally inside the crotch of the pants

Tampon Worn internally, in the vagina. String through vaginal opening allows removal

Mentrual hygiene

- Change a sanitary pad or tampon 3-4 times a day.
- Wash your hands before and after changing pads or tampons.
- Wash your vulva daily from front to back, using plain soap and water. Don't use powder or deodorants.
- To minimize the risk of infection, don't wear tampons overnight.
- You may want to wait a few months before you try tampons.

IF PERIODS STOP

- A missed period could mean you're pregnant. See pages 62–3 and 76 for advice on contraception and how to cope with a pregnancy.
- Periods may stop altogether if your weight falls below 98lbs (45kg), as in anorexia, or if your muscle-to-fat ratio is too high, as when training hard for sports.

You need medical advice on either of these interruptions to the normal function of your body.

Painful periods

Some pain during a period is common, but very painful periods (dysmenorrhea) should be treated by your doctor.

. . celebration of being FEMALE.

HOW BOYS WORK

Be **AWARE** of how your body is *changing*

Boys are affected by *hormones* just as much as **GIRLS**

See also "How Girls Work," page 20

THINK ABOUT...

The speed at which your body changes at puberty may take you by surprise. The changes take place when your testes begin making the male sex hormone testosterone. Testosterone also triggers sperm production and makes you sexually aware. You'll begin to get erections because your penis is more sensitive to touch, or because you become excited by something or someone you see.

WORRIES AND QUESTIONS...

Most boys worry about the size of their penis, but the size of a person's body parts has nothing to do with how well they work. All boys develop in different ways and at different rates, so it really doesn't mean much to see another boy in the shower with a bigger penis than you. Also, size when soft has no relation to size when erect. In

fact, the truth is often just the opposite; small penises seem to get bigger when erect than large penises. But, most importantly, remember that girls aren't very interested in size – a big penis doesn't make you a better lover.

Wet dreams
When sperm production begins, sperm collect in the seminal vesicles (see opposite). Wet dreams act as a safety valve; the pressure builds up to the extent that you may ejaculate in your sleep – that's why it's called a "wet dream." You may be embarrassed when you have a wet dream, but it's completely normal – all boys have them – and they usually stop as you mature physically.

Circumcision
Removal of the foreskin, the protective layer of flexible skin on the penis, is called circumcision. Circumcision is a simple operation and may be done for religious or medical reasons, but it doesn't affect the way the penis works.

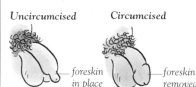

Uncircumcised — foreskin in place *Circumcised* — foreskin removed

REMEMBER... Wet dreams are NORMAL.

HOW YOUR BODY CHANGES

Boys' bodies start to change at 11 to 12 years; their voices "break," and they begin to grow body hair at 14 to 15. Most boys will have to start shaving at 16 or 17.

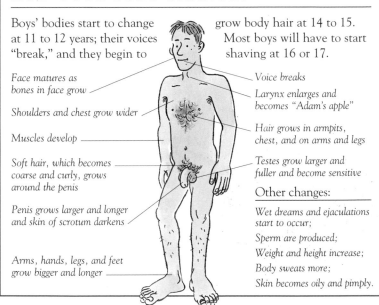

Face matures as bones in face grow

Shoulders and chest grow wider

Muscles develop

Soft hair, which becomes coarse and curly, grows around the penis

Penis grows larger and longer and skin of scrotum darkens

Arms, hands, legs, and feet grow bigger and longer

Voice breaks

Larynx enlarges and becomes "Adam's apple"

Hair grows in armpits, chest, and on arms and legs

Testes grow larger and fuller and become sensitive

Other changes:

Wet dreams and ejaculations start to occur;
Sperm are produced;
Weight and height increase;
Body sweats more;
Skin becomes oily and pimply.

SPERM PRODUCTION

Once a boy starts to produce sperm, he is fertile, which means he could father a child if he has unprotected sex.

Prostate gland
Produces fluid; the mixture is called semen.

Seminal vesicles
Produces fluid that is combined with sperm.

Sperm takes this route

Seminal vesicles

Prostate gland

Testes

Urethra

Vas deferens

Erect penis
At ejaculation, semen travels up through the urethra in short spurts.

Vas deferens
Sperm travel up this long tube before being combined with the fluid.

Testes
Sperm take about two months to mature in the testes.

GETTING HELP

● You may find it difficult to talk about the problems of adolescence for fear of losing face. But try to overcome this fear – most family and friends will be sympathetic.
● Read books on the subject or ask your doctor for information.

● A teacher or guidance counselor may be able to help, or can advise you where to go for help.
● If possible talk to your father, an older brother, or a male relative. Ask him about his adolescence and how he dealt with any problems.

. . all boys have them.

NEW FEELINGS

HORMONAL changes can affect your *mood*

All young people **EXPERIENCE** these *changes*

You feel *miserable* and confused, but it's **NORMAL**

YO-YO SYNDROME

As your body changes, you'll also start to experience new feelings. You may feel shy because you're so conscious of your body, and you may be easily embarrassed because you think people are looking at you. In addition, your moods swing up and down like a yo-yo – you're laughing one minute and crying the next. This is all perfectly normal, and it is caused by the uneven outpouring of sex hormones (see pages 20 and 24). Things will settle down eventually.

WANTING TO BE LEFT ALONE

For a while you'll find that your attitude toward your family and friends may be affected. You may want to be alone more often; sometimes you may not even want the company of your friends. You'll find you need time to sort out all the ideas, problems, and solutions that you've been churning over in your mind. You may think that you're unique, that everyone else can cope but you. But all teenagers are going through the same thing; some just put on a brave act.

DEALING WITH DESIRE

Sexual desire makes such an untimely entrance in a teenager's life. Just as you begin to feel attracted to the opposite sex, you find that your emotions are all over the place and you're feeling really anxious about your body. This can make your feelings about boys or girls difficult to understand. You may want to spend more time with a particular person, but feel too shy and lost for words to make a move.

CONFIDE IN A FRIEND

You'll want to share your feelings with someone who understands (see opposite). Your mixed emotions are not the end of the world, even though they feel like it at times. You're learning to cope with life's ups and downs, and this is a valuable lesson. It helps to compare notes with a close friend, someone you can confide in.

REMEMBER... "Feeling is THINKING"...

GETTING HELP. . .

● Support from a group of friends gives you lots of opinions to benefit from, but beware of any bragging and boasting. People love to exaggerate, so don't believe everything you hear.

● Talk to family and friends who are in their late teens. They can still remember how they felt when they were your age.

● If you're close to your parents, ask if there was a time when they felt as mixed-up as you do. You'll almost certainly find there was.

● There may be someone you can talk to at school: a guidance counselor, or sympathetic teacher.

DO'S AND DON'TS

BE POSITIVE
Do think about the times when you've triumphed.

BE ACTIVE
Do try to take the initiative.

TAKE CARE
Don't let your actions hurt anyone along the way.

BE CAUTIOUS
Don't expect everyone to return your feelings.

FEELING DOWN

"Right Becky, tidy up this room or you're grounded for a week."

"I'm totally depressed. I wish I had someone to talk to."

"Mom says I've got to clean up or she'll ground me. Can you believe it?"

"Why don't I come over and help you, and we can talk while we work."

. . Don't be ashamed of it.

MEETS GIRL

· ·

New kinds of friendship

During your teens, you become increasingly attracted to people of the opposite sex or the same sex. Because you're at an age when you feel so self-conscious, you may be desperate to get to know someone, but too shy to make the first move. Everyone feels this way, but there is a trick and it really works. Look the person in the eye and let your sincere interest show through naturally, without being forced. Start a conversation by asking questions. Go on – try it!

I didn't expect to feel this great. He's terrific. Wait till I tell my friends!

WHAT GIRLS LOOK FOR
· ·

Girls look for **FRIENDSHIP** from boys before *sex*

Girls want boyfriends who are **SENSITIVE**, not *macho*

A sense of **HUMOR** is more *important* than looks

PRIORITIES FOR TEENAGE GIRLS

Many adults think that teenagers are preoccupied with sex but that is simply not true. Nor is sex the greatest influence on your life. Girls ranked the following activities in this order of importance in response to a questionnaire:

- Having close friendships with other girls;
- Doing well at school;
- Having friendships with boys;
- Being romantically involved with a boy;
- Sports;
- A sexual relationship with a boy.

The results of this questionnaire hold both good and bad news for boys: Bad news if you think that girls want a lot of sex – frankly, they prefer sports; good news if you're the kind of boy who simply wants to be friends and go slowly. Romance is important for girls.

THINK ABOUT. . .

Sex is at the bottom of the girls' priority list – intercourse is the least important activity of the choices they could make. Make no mistake: In early adolescence, friendships with other girls are more important to girls than those with boys. As girls go through their teenage years, however, relationships with boys play a greater part in their lives. This is reassuring news for both sexes; it means you don't have to think about sex for some time. It also means that when you hear friends boasting about having had sex, it's probably a lie. You don't need to feel pressured to be like them.

WORRIES AND QUESTIONS. . .

The list of qualities that girls look for in boys (right), should help quell boys' anxieties. It shows that girls aren't looking for movie star looks, scintillating conversation, or expensive entertainment. Most of them are looking for an ordinary boy like you. It's a relief for boys to know they don't have to keep up a macho image. Girls usually prefer boys with a sensitive side – who aren't afraid to show affection.

REMEMBER... Girls PREFER boys ....

GIVING PEOPLE SPACE

"Hi, Susie. Hi, Jane. Let's get together at the coffee shop in an hour or so."

Adam's so patient.

"Oh look, there's Jane! Do you mind if I sit with her for a while – girl talk!"

He always makes my friends feel welcome.

"Don't worry, take your time. I'm happy to chill for a while."

"See you guys at the pool later then."

GIRLS WANT BOYS TO BE . . .

INTELLIGENT
Good conversation and a sense of humor are both important.

NICE LOOKING
A good body is always desirable, but you don't have to be outstandingly handsome.

HONEST
Girls prefer boys who want a genuine relationship, not just a sexual one.

CONFIDENT
Tread this line carefully. Being confident is not the same as being conceited!

SENSIBLE
Girls prefer boys who take good care of themselves, who don't drink to excess or take any drugs.

GENTLE
You shouldn't feel that you have to show off or prove anything to her.

WARNING . . .
Aggression and verbal abuse drive most girls away; forcing yourself on a girl shows lack of respect and is an obvious sign of immaturity. Remember, "no" means "no."

. . who are interesting, not pushy.

WHAT BOYS LOOK FOR

FRIENDSHIPS with girls are more *important* than sex

Boys prefer **PERSONALITY** to good looks

Sexual experience **DOESN'T** make you *more attractive*

PRIORITIES FOR TEENAGE BOYS

When it comes to girls and sexual experience, it's not unusual for teenage boys to have an inferiority complex because they think that all their friends are ahead of them. From the way boys talk, they do put a lot of emphasis on sex, and make out that they spend a lot of time engaged in some kind of sexual activity. But it is just talk! Response to a questionnaire shows that teenage boys give the following activities these priorities:

- Doing well at school;
- Having friendships with other teenage boys;
- Having friendships with girls;
- Sports;
- Being romantically involved with a girl;
- A sexual relationship with a girl.

It's interesting to see how high a priority is given to sports – and something of a relief! Sports activities provide boys with another outlet for their energy.

SEX ISN'T EVERYTHING

"That match has finished me off! I made it with this really sexy girl last night."

"Come on, let's show this to Kathie. She's a sports fan too."

REMEMBER... Being ATTRACTIVE ..

THINK ABOUT. . .

Despite what you may hear, the list of priorities (opposite) shows that for boys sex is one of the least important things in their lives, and that in the early teenage years, friendships with other boys are more important than any kind of friendship with a girl. Girls who are anxious about what boys might expect of them can therefore feel confident that most boys simply want friendship, not sex.

WORRIES AND QUESTIONS. . .

Girls should feel reassured by the list of qualities that boys look for (right). What it's really saying is be yourself – have no pretentions. Be a bit of a clown if you feel like it, but don't be afraid to be serious about the things that matter to you. The list also suggests that boys are more insecure than they'd have girls think, despite all the show. Both boys and girls need kindness and reassurance to bolster their self-esteem.

BOYS WANT GIRLS TO BE . . .

ATTRACTIVE
You don't have to look like a supermodel to be attractive.

RESPONSIVE
Say that you care.

INTELLIGENT
Smart girls can be a turn-on.

WITTY
Funny without being cutting.

HONEST
Don't play games or tease.

NEXT TIME . . .

If you're anxious about making the right impression with boys, talk to your mother or another sensible adult woman who'll be honest with you.

"Hi, Kathie. We've got tickets for Sunday's game. Want to come?"

"You bet! I'll give you a call, and we can all arrange to meet."

. . is about who you are, not how you look.

SOMEONE SPECIAL

The *best* relationships grow out of **FRIENDSHIP**

Deeper involvement means **GIVING** as well as *taking*

Think about what **YOU** have to *offer*

GETTING IN DEEP

Though you've probably been interested in the idea of "going out" with someone since early puberty, this dream may not become a reality until much later. Not all friendships go on to become deep friendships, nor should they. Some are best left light, informal, and nonsexual, and they are just as precious.

You'll know when you want to get more deeply involved, because you'll want to see that particular person more often than anyone else. Because involvement brings responsibilities, you'll have to give some serious consideration as to whether you really want a deeper, closer relationship.

WORRIES AND QUESTIONS. . .

A good relationship makes you feel that you're wanted and needed but it's not exclusive – it shouldn't cut you off from seeing other friends or doing things that are important to you. You should enjoy the time you spend together; the security of your relationship should build your self-esteem.

However, if the relationship isn't going well and you're feeling bad about yourself, it may help to remind yourself of your rights (see below). For instance, if you're regretting something you said or did, it's good to remember that you have the right to make mistakes and learn from them.

A BILL OF RIGHTS FOR PARTNERS

Each partner in a relationship has the right:

- To have opinions
- To affection
- To be trusted
- To security
- To support
- To talk
- To be cared for

- To see friends
- To see family
- To be listened to
- To time alone
- To make mistakes
- To have fun
- To faithfulness

- To respect
- To tolerance
- To show feelings
- To ask for help
- To say "no"
- To religious beliefs
- To patience

REMEMBER...You may not get it RIGHT

WHAT TO AIM FOR IN A RELATIONSHIP

Think about what you have to offer someone in a relationship and make a list; there are lots of qualities that you can offer your new partner, long before sex is on the agenda. Don't forget a relationship requires input from both sides, and that you'll have to put a lot of effort into it. Then compile another list of what you'd like in a boyfriend or girlfriend. But don't set impossible standards, or you could find yourself waiting forever!

What I can offer

- Fun
- Understanding
- Support
- Respect
- Happiness
- Help with problems
- Togetherness
- Love
- Company
- Trust
- Patience
- Sense of humor

Use the two lists as a starting guide, then, once you have established a relationship, look back at your list of "likes" and see just how close you've come to your original ideal.

What I would like

- Someone I can have a good laugh with
- Someone to go out dancing with
- Someone I can really talk to
- Someone to lean on
- Someone to care for
- Someone who won't mind me crying
- Someone who really understands me
- Someone who won't get jealous

. . first time – but that's so for everyone.

HOW TO APPROACH BOYS

• •

Think about **PERSONALITY** rather than *looks*

Don't be **AFRAID** to make the *first move*

Make your opener a *compliment*, even if it's **JOKEY**

THINK ABOUT. . .

These days, girls can more or less call the shots if they want to approach a boy. Gone are the days when it wasn't thought to be proper for girls to make the first move. On the contrary, most boys will be flattered by a girl's interest, and many will be grateful.

If there's someone you'd like to approach, but feel that you don't have the courage, it may help to remember that boys are often much more nervous about making the first move than girls are. The trick is to stay low-key, but not offhand; casual, but not so laid back that he doesn't pick up on your signals at all (see opposite).

Some girls worry about getting a "bad reputation" if they make the first move with a boy, but I suspect this is really fear of rejection. Rejection will happen sometimes, but you'll learn to cope with it.

WORRIES AND QUESTIONS. . .

Here are the answers to some of those questions you've been asking yourself about that boy you like:

● *"Why hasn't he asked me out?"*
Because he's too shy.
● *"Will I be tongue-tied?"*
Not if you plan what to say. It helps to have a few small-talk lines in mind (see page 40).
● *"What if I blush?"*
There's nothing wrong with blushing. Remember, he's probably just as nervous as you are!
● *"How will I know if he likes me?"*
He'll either stay and talk or he'll make an obvious excuse to get away. Don't worry, you won't be left in any doubt either way.

GETTING HELP. . .

● Ask your mother, or your big sister or aunt. They've all been through it before.
● Confide in a friend who won't blab to the whole class. If a boy finds out that you like him from other people, he'll run a mile before you've made the first approach!
● Read teen magazines and books. Although some of the stories are exaggerated, they'll still give you some useful pointers.

REMEMBER... It's all right for YOU . . . . .

MAKING YOUR MOVE

"Steve, can you help me connect up to the Internet?"

"It's quicker on my dad's PC at home. Want to come over later?"

"Here's the address. We'll do some serious surfing tonight."

"Thanks, Steve, see you later!"

DO'S & DON'TS

THE EYES HAVE IT
Don't stare at the floor; make eye contact.

ASK QUESTIONS
Do find out his interests – don't talk sports if he'd rather be surfing the Internet.

STAY COOL
Don't giggle every second sentence. He'll be more impressed by maturity.

BE APPROACHABLE
Don't be an "ice maiden." You'll put him off if you seem too aloof.

MAKE CONTACT
Do touch his arm or shoulder lightly if you think it's appropriate – but don't drape yourself all over him. He'll feel smothered.

BOOST HIS EGO
Do pay him a compliment, even if it's a lighthearted one. That way you'll start a conversation and flatter him.

NEXT TIME . . .
Think about: How he reacted and whether it was what you hoped for; what made it good; and what you might do to build your confidence when you meet again.

. . to take the INITIATIVE.

HOW TO APPROACH GIRLS

Think about the *girl* and not about **YOURSELF**

Show you're **INTERESTED** in her, ask *questions*

Watch how *experienced* **BOYS** approach **GIRLS**

THINK ABOUT. . .

When you approach a girl for the first time, she will probably be as nervous as you, so don't be discouraged if she seems a little off-hand, especially if she's with a group of her friends. Give her time to relax, and think of ways to put her at her ease – she'll be put off if you're aggressive or arrogant. Make your first approach somewhere very casual – sit at her table at lunch, offer to walk her home from the school bus, or speak to her at a place where lots of other young people go, such as a popular coffee shop or fast-food restaurant. Think about the clothes you'll wear – be relaxed, but be yourself. Try to do some discreet research into her interests and family background, and think about some suitable conversation topics in advance so you'll feel a lot more confident yourself.

WORRIES AND QUESTIONS. . .

Everyone worries about being snubbed or put down, or worse, about looking foolish. Tension and worry will tend to make you stammer, so stay as cool and laid-back as you can. Try to pretend that you're talking to a friend you feel completely at ease with. To calm your nerves, repeat to yourself the first couple of things you plan to say and don't be afraid to take the initiative – girls expect that. The best thing you can be is sincere – then you'll show that your interest is genuine.

GETTING HELP. . .

- Ask an older brother, or a friend of your brother, for advice on what to say and do – and on the kind of pitfalls you should avoid.
- Choose a friendly adult, ideally mom or dad; but an aunt, grandparent, or friend of your parents, will do. Explain honestly what your fears are. Then ask for some suggestions based on their wealth of experience.
- Buy or borrow some teen girls' magazines and study them to find out what interests girls. If you have a sister, ask her advice.

REMEMBER... You're at your BEST ......

HOW TO GO ABOUT IT

"Do you mind if I sit here?"

"Would you like to go blading?"

"Yes, okay, I'm free about sixish."

"I'll meet you at the park."

DO'S & DON'TS

LISTEN
Do listen carefully to her and ask her questions.

EYE CONTACT
Don't sit silently, avoiding eye contact – focus your attention on her.

ASK QUESTIONS
Don't start all your sentences with "I"; ask about her. "What do you think about..." is more interesting than "I think..."

BE NATURAL
Don't try too hard to make an impression; be natural.

PRACTICE
Do try out your small-talk line on your sister or a friend's sister; you could ask her if she has any suggestions.

LAUGHTER
Do arm yourself with a couple of good jokes to make her laugh. But make sure they're clean ones!

NEXT TIME . . .
Think about: What went well and plan to emphasize your strengths; what went wrong; what you could have done to salvage the situation; how to avoid it in the future.

. . when you're BEING YOURSELF!

MAKING THE FIRST MOVE

There's only one way to find out if someone likes you – talk to them! Lines are just a handy way to get a conversation going. It really doesn't matter if your opening line is a little corny and obvious; if someone likes you, he or she will be anxious to respond. Watch for a good opportunity to make your pitch.

REMEMBER... Don't waste your CHANCE.

PICK UP LINES FOR ALL OCCASIONS

For example, if the object of your desire has changed his or her appearance in some way, or is engaged in some interesting activity, don't dither – seize the opportunity and use it as an opener. If the person doesn't respond, you won't have lost anything. But you may find that you have everything to gain!

. . . .to get to know someone.

SERIOUS

Thinking about sex

You've fallen madly in love and you're no longer satisfied with furtive glances, or even holding hands. But all that follows in this chapter is not to encourage you to do, but to think. Make sure that you read "Contraception" (page 62) and "Safe Sex" (page 64) twice. Even when your partner wants to share a sexual relationship, there's so much to consider, because you're responsible for your partner's safety as well as their pleasure.

Can't hurt to carry a condom – tonight could be the night!

Looks like I'm gonna be vertically challenged for the rest of this party.

GETTING INVOLVED

Emotional *involvement* comes **BEFORE** sex

Relationships mean *companionship* and **SECURITY**

Involvement brings **RESPONSIBILITY** to *each other*

THE PERFECT PAIR

A good relationship is personally enriching; It provides you with comfort, understanding, and support. You'll feel that you are being loved – and you'll also get a lot of pleasure from giving. While your values may be similar to your partner's, any differences are exciting, and you should be able to respect each other's points of view without any real friction.

Good relationships aren't too "exclusive." They don't block off your involvement in other things that are still important. You enjoy each other's company, but not all of your time together is spent being romantic and sexual. A healthy relationship enables you to enjoy time with other people as well, and it should always build your self-esteem.

WORRIES AND QUESTIONS. . .

A lot of girls need emotional involvement before they can even think about sex; many feel torn between the desire for sexual freedom and the fear that they may get a bad reputation. They may have grown up believing that they shouldn't try sex – let alone enjoy it – so they feel guilty if they do either.

While boys tend to have greater sexual freedom, they don't always enjoy the pressure to be "macho," and they can feel really insecure about having to make the first move. Nowadays, however, it is perfectly acceptable for a girl to ask a boy out if she wants to.

THINK ABOUT. . .

When a friendship is deepening into a close relationship, ask yourself the following:
● Might some aspects of the friendship become uncomfortable if it got more serious?
● Are either of you possessive? Jealousy can reduce a close relationship to misery.
● Would you be able to back off? Knowing when to draw back will save you a good deal of heartache.

REMEMBER...If you think SEX may be . . . .

GETTING CLOSER

" Well Jennifer, I've had a great time, but I suppose this is good-night."

"Yes, I'd better go in... but maybe we can do this again sometime?"

"I'd love to. How about I give you a call the same time next week?

"Perfect! And maybe next time you'll get invited in for coffee."

DO'S AND DON'TS

EXPRESS YOURSELF
Do make a point of telling someone that you like him or her; it's good for you both.

HOLD BACK
Don't try to embrace or kiss someone if you know that he or she doesn't want it.

BE INTERESTED
Do ask for feedback and opinions, and give your friend compliments.

BE PATIENT
Don't force anyone to be intimate; wait until you're both ready and enjoy the friendship in the meantime.

BE SUPPORTIVE
Don't be afraid to lean on each other for support if you're having difficulties at home, school, or work.

STAND BACK
Do give each other the space to spend some time with your own best friends.

NEXT TIME . . .
Think about: Consider the consequences of getting close to a partner long before you reach that stage. Decide what's right and wrong for you, and learn to say "no" (see page 50).

. . on the agenda, CARRY condoms.

SENSITIVE PLACES

Wanting to **TOUCH** someone you like is *natural*

The *"erogenous zones"* are specially **SENSITIVE** areas

CARESSING doesn't work if it's *forced*

EROGENOUS ZONES

There are sensitive places all over the body; they're called erogenous zones. When these zones are touched or caressed, it feels very nice – so nice that you get excited. But it does also depend on who's touching these places. If you like a person very much, being touched anywhere can feel good – even places like your knees and ears. Erogenous zones are more sensitive because the skin in these areas has millions of nerves near the surface, and they're there for a reason: To make procreation attractive (see page 54). Everyone has different erogenous zones, but generally the areas that are most sensitive are:

- Breasts and nipples;
- Buttocks and thighs;
- Outer genital organs.

A boy's penis and a girl's clitoris have the greatest sensitivity of all, but because a girl's vagina has very few nerves inside (in fact, it's almost numb), girls cannot have orgasms there (see pages 60–1).

ONE STEP AT A TIME

"I thought we could just stay in tonight with a video and pizza."

"Sounds great, Paul. What kind of movie did you want to watch?"

REMEMBER...Intimacy is PHYSICAL...

THINK ABOUT. . .

Touching someone intimately is a sign that you like and respect that person. Kissing and stroking should always be thoughtful and caring; this kind of contact doesn't work if it's aggressive or mechanical. You can show a great deal of affection just by caressing a person's face, neck, and shoulders, without ever going near the breasts or genital area. And boys should know that most girls prefer this gentle approach to anything else.

WORRIES AND QUESTIONS. . .

Intimacy makes everyone feel very vulnerable, because you have to reveal yourself. If you're rejected, you end up feeling humiliated and hurt. But, on the positive side, you also have the chance that you will get the response you want. Try to take things gently. Make small, subtle advances and see how the person reacts before you make bigger and bolder moves.

DO'S & DON'TS

LEARN
Do find out about your own body by lying in bed and touching yourself.

GO SLOWLY
Do proceed slowly when touching someone, and ask if it's all right (see below).

BE SURE
Don't be afraid to stop someone from touching you at any stage. If it doesn't feel good, say so.

NEXT TIME . . .

There's no need to be nervous about the next step. Once two people are feeling really close, touching happens as naturally as night follows day.

"Something romantic, of course. Is this okay? Ummm... you don't mind, do you?"

"Of course I don't! Let's not bother with the video after all."

. . and EMOTIONAL.

GETTING CLOSER

INTIMACY means *physical* and *emotional* closeness

As you get *close*, you want to **EXPLORE** each other

Love play is **EXCITING**, even if *sex* isn't on the agenda

When a boy and girl become deeply involved, they'll find that kissing and touching will one day lead to the boy touching the girl's breasts, nipples, and perhaps even her clitoris. And the girl will feel encouraged to touch the boy in his intimate places as well. Love play is more than romance – it's part of the escalating spiral of excitement that makes for satisfying sex.

WORRIES AND QUESTIONS. . .

Most boys feel driven to do anything that will bring about orgasm in the fastest possible way. But girls are quite different. A girl will only welcome her genital organs being stroked and kissed once she has been sufficiently aroused in other ways and she feels comfortable with it. Without the chance to build up a sufficient level of sex hormones through kissing, caressing, and touching (see page 52), sex is not only uncomfortable for a girl, it's undesirable. Most boys don't appreciate how long this can take, since their own level of excitement rises far more quickly. To arouse a girl gently, see opposite.

SET YOUR OWN PACE

Belinda's bragging again ... she makes me feel like such a prude!

"It felt soooo good to be that close to him, I mean – it was intense!"

Perhaps I should have let Ben go further last night.

"If you haven't made love, you haven't lived, know what I'm saying?"

REMEMBER... You may feel CLUMSY...

ATTITUDES TO PETTING

The answers to the following questions illustrate that while boys want to start petting after only a few dates, girls prefer to go slow, and let petting arise out of their feelings for the boy.

	GIRLS	BOYS
When is light petting okay?	When you know each other quite well, after a few dates or weeks.	On the first, second, or third date.
Does everyone enjoy petting?	Only half the girls do.	Nearly all the boys do.
When is heavy petting considered okay?	Usually only when you love the boy, definitely not on the first date.	Boys still think this is okay on the first or second date.
Who should start the petting?	Girls usually wait for the boy to start.	Boys feel pressured to make the first move.

TAKE YOUR TIME

Boys need to be extremely sensitive if they are introducing petting, and not go too far too fast. Most girls enjoy passionate kissing, but may pull back from petting involving the breasts or genital area, unless it is gentle at first. Always stop if she says "no." She means it! (See page 50).

NEXT TIME . . .

Think about: If any aspect of petting makes you feel really uncomfortable, tell your partner to stop, rather than going through the motions because you feel you should.

"Sorry I came on a little strong last night, Judy. You do know I love you?"

"I'd just feel happier if we took things a little more slowly."

. . at first, but things will IMPROVE.

YOU CAN SAY NO

The only reason to have **SEX** is because you *want* to

Deciding to have sex should **NEVER** be taken *lightly*

No one should **EVER** make you have sex

Young people are presented with many difficult choices and pressures to do things that they feel uncomfortable about – taking drugs, drinking alcohol, smoking, and sex. Girls *and* boys need courage to withstand the pressure of the moment; to realize they can say "no" without losing face.

There are lots of reasons why you may feel unsure or uncomfortable about sex. For your own sense of self-respect, don't be pressured into having sex because you think your boyfriend or girlfriend will leave you or be disappointed. You and nobody else decides whether you want to enter a sexual relationship. If you haven't managed to figure out your sexual values yet, then you should say "no."

NO MEANS NO

People can come up with lots of reasons for persuading their partners to have sex when they don't really want to. Typical ploys include saying things like: "If you don't I'll tell everyone you're a tease"; or "You know you want to really"; or "I'll leave you if you don't." It's not acceptable to "trick" your partner in this way – if a person says "no," then you should respect his or her wishes.

WHY GIRLS FIND IT HARD TO SAY NO

Almost every girl has difficulty in saying "no" at some time and finds herself on a date having sexual contact when she doesn't really want it. There are lots of reasons why girls find it difficult to come out and say "no" firmly: the most common is that she doesn't want to hurt the boy's feelings or is afraid of being thought a prude. Some girls may be worried that they're not going along with what other girls appear to be doing.

With all these pressures, it takes a brave girl to say "no," but you must say it if that's what you feel. If your boyfriend really cares for you, he'll agree. On the other hand, you'll lose a lot of self-respect if you say "yes" when you really mean "no."

NEXT TIME . . .
Think about: How you would feel if you went ahead and had sex when you didn't really want to. It's a terrible, desolate feeling of remorse. Decide now you're never going to feel like that.

REMEMBER . . . If you don't want sex. . . . . .

JUST SAY NO

. . be brave and say NO.

BEFORE INTERCOURSE

Love-making needn't **INVOLVE** sexual intercourse

There are *lots* of ways of giving **PLEASURE**

FOREPLAY may even *lead* to an orgasm

I've got all the time in the world to learn to love her.

This has got to be the real thing!

SATISFACTION WITHOUT SEX

In a good sexual relationship, there are many different ways to explore each other's bodies without having actual sexual intercourse. Sex is the proverbial iceberg of which intercourse is only the tip – the one-eighth that's showing above the surface. Foreplay is the seven-eighths that seethes beneath the surface; it can help you to overcome any anxieties that you may have about sex. It can often lead to orgasm, and may even be more fulfilling than full sexual intercourse, particularly for girls who may find it easier to have an orgasm with foreplay than with penetrative sex. See right for some of the possibilities that make up that exciting seven-eighths.

DIFFERENT KINDS OF STIMULATION

Because teenagers regard full sexual intercourse as a huge step (in many states it's against the law to have sex until you've reached your late teens), foreplay and petting often become ends in themselves. This kind of lovemaking is usually just as fulfilling because you can reach orgasm in the following ways:

● Mutual masturbation is when you stroke and rub each other's genital organs. Girls stroke or rub their boyfriend's penis, while boys stroke their girlfriend's clitoris.

● Oral sex is when you kiss, lick, nuzzle, and suck each other's genital organs: girls do it to the penis (fellatio); boys do it to the clitoris (cunnilingus).

● "69" is when a boy and a girl perform fellatio and cunnilingus for each other at the same time; you may even climax at the same time (simultaneous orgasm).

● Simultaneous orgasm is possible if a boy rubs a girl's clitoris with his penis; he should still wear a condom, as semen can enter the vagina, even without penetration.

● For lesbian and homosexual sex, see pages 86–9.

see pages 86–9.

REMEMBER... Sex is just one way . . . .

WORRIES AND QUESTIONS. . .

Early sexual experiences can be as daunting as they are exciting. Here are some answers to questions you might be asking yourself:

● *"Is something wrong with my body if I don't have an orgasm?"*
Sex is such a complex act, that the likelihood of your early sexual experiences being satisfying are slim. But don't worry – this has nothing to do with the size or shape of your genital organs, whether you're a boy or a girl.
● *"Are boys always lucky enough to have an orgasm?"*
Just because boys ejaculate doesn't mean that they always have an explosive orgasm as well. It might have been rather disappointing, and he may be feeling frustrated and inadequate, though he's probably too shy to discuss this with you.
● *"What if my partner wants to have oral sex but I'm not sure?"*
If you feel shy about this, start gently and slowly, so that you can respond to and guide each other. But stop if it feels uncomfortable.

HOW YOU REALLY FEEL ABOUT LOVE

CASUAL SEX
Contrary to popular opinion, most teenagers aren't casual about sex, and instead have very responsible views on it.

COMMITMENT
Emotional and romantic commitment to your girlfriend or boyfriend is something most of you need to feel before you have sex.

TRUE LOVE
Most girls and around 50 percent of boys want to be in love before they'll have sex with their partners.

AFFECTION
Because you care so deeply about your sexual activities, you see sex as a way of expressing mutual love and affection – and reject the idea of sex as a purely physical act.

. . of expressing love and affection.

SEXUAL INTERCOURSE

*Bi*ologically, intercourse is for **REPRODUCTION**

Understanding **EXACTLY** what is going on is *important*

Knowing about sex makes it **SAFER** and more *enjoyable*

THINK ABOUT. . .

You may think you know all about how sex works, but it's surprising how many people – even adults who have had children – have a very sketchy idea about what really happens during sexual intercourse. Knowing exactly what happens, and why, is the best way to avoid the unwelcome outcomes of sex such as unwanted pregnancy or sexual disease (see pages 70–81). It's no use getting good advice on safe sexual practices if you don't understand why they are needed. So, if you think you know it all already, use this information as revision. For those who are less sure, remember that you are being smart in taking time to find out.

WHAT SEX IS FOR

When it come to biology, sexual intercourse is the means by which we reproduce. But when it comes to relationships, it's a way to convey love, providing a lasting bond between couples – as well as the joy of raising a family. When you're young, you are just beginning to explore your sexuality.

THE MECHANICS OF SEX

For sexual intercourse to be successful, both partners need to be fully aroused, usually by foreplay: Holding, caressing, and kissing. The senses are stimulated and changes occur in the genital area. Sexual arousal happens all over the body, but because boys get aroused much faster than girls, they should wait for a girl to "catch up," so that both partners can enjoy sex.

PENETRATIVE SEXUAL INTERCOURSE

When the boy inserts his penis into the girl's vagina, rhythmic movement increases stimulation of the penis in order for the boy to reach orgasm. The girl's clitoris, however, often fails to get stimulated during penetrative sex. The boy ejaculates as he reaches a climax, when semen spurts out of the penis to be deposited high inside the vagina. Then the penis goes limp, and the clitoris shrinks.

Vagina
Lubricating fluid keeps the vaginal walls moist.

Clitoris
Though the clitoris may be stimulated, penetrative sex often fails to achieve orgasm.

Clitoris

Semen travels through the urethra during ejaculation

Erect penis
Blood fills the spongy tissue of the penis to make it stiff.

Vaginal wall
The walls of the vagina expand to accommodate the penis.

Vaginal wall

WHAT HAPPENS DURING SEX

GIRLS

- Heartbeat and breathing accelerate; you feel hot.

- Skin becomes pinker, with a blotchy rash, which is normal.

- Blood flow increases to the genital organs which swell; nipples become erect.

- The clitoris enlarges slightly as it becomes filled with blood.

- Vagina secretes lubricating mucus to ease penetration.

- Excitement will be felt as a warm, tingling sensation in the genital area.

- You may have an orgasm.

BOYS

- Heartbeat and breathing increase; you feel hot.

- Blood flow increases, particularly to genital organs.

- Nipples, testes, and scrotal skin become very sensitive to the touch.

- Penis becomes erect as blood fills the spongy tissue. Blood is prevented from leaving by a one-way valve.

- Excitement will be felt as warm tingling sensations in the genital area, climaxing during ejaculation.

- You may have an orgasm.

.. contraception and S A F E sex.

THE FIRST TIME

It's right to feel **NERVOUS**, it's a *huge* step

Only **YOU** can decide if you're *ready*

Be **REALISTIC** in your expectations, not *idealistic*

THE POWER OF SEXUAL DESIRE

Sexual desire is an overpowering feeling. When you're attracted to someone, you feel as if you're being drawn helplessly toward a magnet. And because you can't stop daydreaming about him or her, this can really affect your concentration, whether you're studying or working. You'll want to be close to the person, and you'll find that your body reacts by feeling excited, and nervous. All of this may lead to sex – or it may not. When you do finally have sexual intercourse with someone for the first time, it will be a significant moment. So try to have an element of control when you get swept away by passion; choose to share this moment with a boy or girl who means something to you.

FEELING EMBARRASSED

Some young people shy away from the fun aspects of foreplay and sex because they feel so embarrassed about their bodies. This can be a real problem for girls because not only do they have to overcome any early conditioning about sexual activity being "wrong," they may also have negative (and totally unfounded) feelings about their genital organs being "dirty." One reason that boys usually feel more confident is because they have been brought up to believe that their penis is something to be proud of. As you and your partner get to know each other's responses better, you'll feel far less inhibited, and then the "play" in foreplay (see page 52) can have free rein. Foreplay is essential to successful sexual intercourse.

"I'm worried that you won't find me attractive after this."

GIRLS' WORRIES

● *"Will it be painful?"*
Intercourse is rarely painful the first time, because the hymen (the membrane inside the vaginal opening) has nearly always broken during active sports such as horse riding or gymnastics. If you have started to use tampons, these can help to break it, too. When sexual intercourse is approached gently, after plenty of foreplay, it should not hurt at all.

● *"What if I don't enjoy it?"*
Many girls find that their first time fails to live up to their romantic expectations; it may even lack excitement. If this happens to you, it doesn't mean that there's anything wrong with you. Sexual satisfaction takes time and experience between partners.

● *"What will people think if they find out I'm no longer a virgin?"*
One of the biggest blocks to sexual satisfaction is being consumed with feelings of guilt about having sexual intercourse. If you have any doubts, don't do it. But remember that sex is a natural and enjoyable act between two people who love each other. Try to learn to let go and give yourself permission to enjoy sex.

NEXT TIME . . .

In the early stages of sexual experience, both boys and girls may feel awkward and shy. It takes time to have good sex, so learn to communicate and be patient with each other.

PRIORITIZE YOUR PREFERENCES

You can resist all kinds of pressure if you give your own preferences priority. Try a few of these responses; they're suitable for both sexes.

"There are a lot of things I like doing other than sex."

"I know you've got your own values, but I've got mine, and they're important to me."

"It's very easy to have sex, but I want more than that."

"An orgasm isn't everything."

"I'm not the one behaving like a child. It's childish not to consider the consequences of having sex."

"I can't just turn myself on whenever you want me to."

I want to be sure we're doing this for the right reasons.

"I'm not sure I'm ready to go all the way. Can we talk a little first?"

. . isn't an EXAM that you pass or fail.

THE FIRST TIME *continued*

IT'S NEVER A CASUAL DECISION

There's only one reason for having sex, and that's because you want to. Not because all your friends are having sex; not because most television shows would have you believe that people are always jumping into bed together at the drop of a hat; and not because your partner is putting pressure on you. Deciding whether you want to have sex is one of the hardest decisions you'll ever have to make,

and you'll need to do some soul-searching first. Try to explore your feelings and values; encourage your partner to do the same.

Sex is the ultimate expression of love – without love it can be a form of exploitation that leaves you feeling empty and hurt. If you have any doubts at all, wait until the time – and the partner – are right. Below, you'll find some suggestions for questions that you can ask your partner; they may help you decide if he or she is right for you.

QUESTIONING YOUR PARTNER'S SEXUAL VALUES

LOVE
- Do you see sex as an act of love?
- Do you love me?

COMMITMENT
- What does sex mean to you?
- In what ways will having sex change our relationship?
- How will my saying "no" change our relationship?

SETTING LIMITS
- Will you respect my right to set limits to the way we have sex?
- If I feel really uncomfortable about something, will you stop?

SAFETY
- Do you believe in safe sex?
- Are you prepared to take responsibility for contraception?

Why don't they just get on with it?

I want this to really mean something.

"How do you really feel about me, Sue? It's important for me to know."

REMEMBER... Your first time doesn't . . . . .

BOYS' WORRIES

● *"How well can I expect to perform the first time I have sex?"*

Faced with your first full sexual encounter, you're naturally going to feel nervous, especially if you think your partner expects you to know exactly what to do. You can help yourself to get over this by trying not to be in too much of a hurry. Allow plenty of time for foreplay, and make sure your partner enjoys this by asking her how she feels. Remember, it's not a race.

● *"Will it be really easy for me to have an orgasm?"*

You're much more likely to have an orgasm at the climax of sexual intercourse than your girlfriend is. In fact, until you've had more experience, you may find this happens faster than you expected. Once you've climaxed, however, you'll probably feel a great sense of relief. You'll also begin to feel more confident.

● *"What if my girlfriend doesn't really enjoy having sex?"*

If your girlfriend doesn't have an orgasm at first (it's much harder for girls to have an orgasm during penetrative sexual intercourse), this doesn't mean that you've failed as a lover, or that she hasn't enjoyed the closeness and intimacy of the experience. You can help build your girlfriend's confidence by exploring other forms of sexual contact with her, such as mutual masturbation and oral sex (see page 52). Always ask her what she likes and dislikes.

I must make him realize I'm happy just being close.

I hope she isn't expecting the performance of a lifetime.

"I want this moment to be perfect for both of us, but it's my first time, too."

GETTING HELP. . .

● The most obvious people to talk to and question are your closest friends; not acquaintances, but real friends with whom you can share confidences.

● If you have a close enough relationship, talk to an older brother, sister, or cousin who has sexual experience.

● Even though friends can offer advice and reassurance, if you find your sexual experience difficult or unfulfilling, you can only hope to improve matters by talking to your partner. Try to talk openly without embarrassment – before, during, and after the experience.

NEXT TIME . . .

Think about: Get to know your partner really well before you embark on a sexual relationship, so that you're comfortable enough with each other to talk things through.

. . set your sexual AGENDA for life.

EXPLAINING ORGASM

Orgasm is *easier* for boys than for **GIRLS**

DON'T see intercourse as the *main* event

It helps if you *understand* each other's **BODIES**

ORGASM AND BOYS

It isn't difficult for boys to achieve orgasm; in fact, at the start of their sexual life, most have difficulty in controlling themselves when they are very excited. Boys have usually masturbated long before they ever become involved with a girl, so they know what to expect. Boys can reach orgasm in several ways: manual or oral stimulation by someone else; masturbation; and sexual intercourse.

WHY IT'S DIFFERENT FOR GIRLS

It's more problematic for girls because many are unsure whether they've had an orgasm; a female orgasm doesn't have such a dramatic ending as a male one. Girls also react differently according to whether they're being stimulated by a hand, mouth, or penis (see page 52).

UNDERSTANDING GIRLS' BODIES

Intercourse on its own isn't always successful in bringing a girl to orgasm. She needs to have her clitoris stimulated, but intercourse only stimulates the vagina (see page 55), which isn't usually enough to bring about orgasm – though most men think it is! Many girls who've had sexual intercourse have never had an orgasm, and only a quarter of girls manage to have orgasms with any frequency. But all of these girls can achieve orgasm through masturbation or manual stimulation by their boyfriends. There is absolutely nothing wrong with a girl who cannot have an orgasm through sexual intercourse. It's the sex that's at fault, not the girl.

Sex is great when you can tell each other what you want.

I'm so lucky to have a boyfriend who wants to please me.

"It's such a relief that we can talk about sex like this together, Jennifer."

REMEMBER... Intercourse is not necessarily

GETTING IT TOGETHER

BEING INVOLVED
Girls who find it easiest to have an orgasm are those who are very involved with their boyfriends and find them very exciting.

BEING RELAXED
Girls are more relaxed about sex if they've explored their own responses through masturbation.

GETTING AROUSED
Girls need direct physical stimulation of the clitoris to achieve orgasm.

KEEPING IT GOING
Interruption of physical stimulation can prevent a girl from reaching orgasm; sexual stimulation should always continue to a natural climax.

BEING FRANK
Girls who can talk openly about their sexual needs usually achieve orgasm; boys wish such frankness was more common.

SEX TALK
If you talk to each other during lovemaking, you get to know one another in a very deep way.

EXPLODING MYTHS
It's a myth that there's more than one kind of female orgasm. Research shows that there is only one type, centered on the clitoris.

ENJOYING YOURSELVES
The most important thing is to enjoy sex, whether you achieve orgasm through intercourse or manual stimulation.

NOTHING WILL AROUSE A GIRL IF SHE DOESN'T LIKE THE BOY

. . the most rewarding FORM of sex.

CONTRACEPTION

Contraception **PREVENTS** unwanted *pregnancies*

Contraception is the *responsibility* of **BOTH** partners

ALL young people should *know* about contraception

THINK ABOUT. . .

Whatever you do – don't wait until you're having sex to seek advice on contraception. Make sure that you're well informed beforehand. Contrary to what many adults think, there is no evidence to back up the belief that explicit information about sex and contraception encourages young people to be promiscuous and experimental. In fact, the reverse is true – the more informed you are, the more responsible you can be. Unfortunately, there are still thousands of teenage pregnancies every year. Don't add to this depressing and unnecessary statistic.

If you decide to have full sexual intercourse, use a reliable method of contraception (see opposite). Remember, the responsibility for contraception is shared with your boyfriend or girlfriend.

GETTING HELP. . .

● Ideally you should get contraceptive advice from your parents (see below). The topic is less likely to upset them if you broach the subject *before* you enter into a sexual relationship.
● If you find it difficult to confide in your parents on sexual matters, visit your doctor, or a family planning center.

TALK ABOUT IT

Talk about condoms with mom! How embarrassing!

That was much easier than I thought!

That's put my mind at ease.

"Would it be a good idea to think about contraception now you're going steady?"

"Thanks, mom, you've been a big help. Don't worry, I'm going to be responsible."

REMEMBER . . . The best contraceptive is . . .

FACTS ABOUT CONTRACEPTION

A girl can STILL get pregnant:

- If penetration doesn't take place. Leaking sperm can still reach a girl's vagina if the penis makes close contact.
- If a boy promises to "be careful" by withdrawing his penis just before he ejaculates. He may even promise not to ejaculate, but don't believe him!
- If she avoids sex during ovulation (so-called natural contraception).
- If she has sex during a period; ovulation can happen shortly after the period begins if she has an irregular menstrual cycle.
- If it's the first time she has ever had full intercourse.
- If she hasn't had an orgasm.
- If she washes out her vagina (douches) after sex.

METHODS OF CONTRACEPTION

Avoiding sex during ovulation isn't a reliable form of contraception. Below are various types of contraception that are more effective in preventing pregnancy if used according to instructions.

Illustration	**The Pill**
combined pill *mini-pill*	99% effective. Combined pill contains progestogen and estrogen; mini-pill is progestogen only. Obtainable from family planning center or doctor.
male condom *female condom*	**Condom** 98% effective. Fits over erect penis or inside vagina, as appropriate. Widely available from a variety of retail outlets. Protects against STDs. Never reuse.
diaphragm *spermicidal cream*	**Diaphragm** 93% effective. Fits around cervix. Always use with spermicidal cream. Reusable. Fitted by doctor or family planning center.
intra–uterine device (IUD)	**IUD** 98% effective. Only for women who have had a baby. A small device is inserted vaginally into womb by doctor or nurse.
morning-after pill	**Morning-after pill** Must be taken within 72 hours of sexual intercourse. Available from some family planning centers and doctors.

. . . a sense of RESPONSIBILITY.

SAFE SEX

Safe sex helps *protect* you from **STDs** and **HIV/AIDS**

Safe sex *means* being **RESPONSIBLE** about sex

ALWAYS practice safe sex, *nothing* less will do

CONDOMS AND STDs

In order for sex to be safe from STDs, you should wear a condom for all forms of penetrative sex – vaginal, anal, and oral. Make sure that you know how to use one properly and only use condoms that are made from latex or polyurethane. Never use condoms from out-of-date packages since they can deteriorate and even burst.

YOUR RIGHTS

Demanding safe sex is your right. If your partner resents this, he or she is not thinking about you, and you should question your relationship. If your partner won't use a condom, you should refuse to have sex and consider ending the relationship. By acting irresponsibly, he or she puts you in danger. (See page 50 for everyone's right to say "no.")

HOW TO USE A CONDOM

1. Remove condom from the package carefully - pinch tip to remove air.

2. Holding the tip, roll the condom over the penis when it's fully erect.

3. Roll condom down to base of penis, to prevent semen leaking.

4. After ejaculation, remove at once, before penis becomes soft.

HOW TO USE A FEMALE CONDOM

 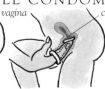 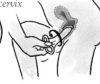

vagina   *cervix*

1. Pinch closed end with your fingers to flatten the condom rim.

2. Raise one knee. Slide closed end into your vagina, as far as it will go.

3. Check condom is in place. Lower ring fits outside vaginal entrance.

4. Pinch the outer ring to remove; twist to prevent semen escaping.

REMEMBER... Whatever you do . . . .

YOUR RESPONSIBILITIES

I want to show her that I care.

I want peace of mind.

"Let's use a condom, then we can both relax and enjoy sex."

PREVENTING PREGNANCY TOO

While condoms are great for safe sex, don't entirely rely on them to prevent pregnancy. Semen can leak if you haven't managed to use the condom correctly, or if you've used an out-of-date one. It's best for girls to be either on the pill, or to use a diaphragm as well. See pages 62–3 for advice.

GETTING HELP. . .

● Your doctor or family planning center will gladly give you information on condoms.
● A whole variety of condoms are available, and some of them have been designed to make sex a little more interesting! Condoms are available at supermarkets, pharmacies, and even some public bathrooms.
● You can get advice on safe sex practices from AIDS charities, hospitals, and gay hotlines (see page 92 for useful addresses).

DO'S AND DON'TS

CARRY A CONDOM
Do carry a condom with you at all times, girls as well as boys.

PRACTICE FIRST
Do make sure you know how to use a condom before you have sex with someone.

CONDOMS EVERY TIME
Do use a condom until you're absolutely sure there's no risk to or from your partner.

ONCE ONLY
Don't ever try to use a condom more than once.

BE FRANK
Do be open about previous sexual experiences when you start a relationship, and tell your partner about any chronic infections, such as herpes.

NO CASUAL SEX
Don't have sex with someone you hardly know and may never meet again, such as at a party, or on vacation.

NEXT TIME . . .

Don't drop your guard for a moment; always practice safe sex. You want to be able to relax when you have sex; you don't want to have to worry about pregnancy and STDs.

. . DON'T take chances with your life.

IF YOU BREAK UP

Feelings can **CHANGE** with little *warning*

Ending an affair can be painful for **BOTH** partners

No one can be **FORCED** to *return* affection

THINK ABOUT. . .

As you begin to enjoy the closeness and security that comes with being involved with someone, you also run the risk of breaking up one day. A short-term, uncomplicated fling can be fun, and can end without regrets for either of you. But if a relationship is deeper, particularly if it develops into a full sexual relationship, a breakup is going to be painful. It may seem like the end of the world, but there's not a lot you can do about it. You can't make someone return your affection if he or she doesn't feel it anymore, so try to bow out gracefully. Whatever you do, don't go knocking on a closed door.

YOU WILL GET OVER IT

Breaking up can be like a bereavement; it's very painful and can leave you feeling abandoned and full of negative thoughts about yourself. It's something that happens to most people at some stage in their lives. You'll be a stronger person for the experience. And you will fall in love again.

THINK POSITIVELY

- A breakup doesn't mean that you're a failure. Your partner is equally responsible.
- Keep believing in yourself.
- Don't be afraid to get support from close friends and family if you're feeling really miserable.

COPING WITH A BREAK UP

I'm gonna have to put this behind me.

Phew, I told her at last.

I'm sure she still loves me deep down.

What did I ever see in him?

✔ **"He wasn't worth it. You're better off without him!"**

✗ **"Won't you go out with me just one more time?"**

REMEMBER... Everyone has had . . . .

IF YOU END A RELATIONSHIP

If you're the one who is ending a relationship, you owe it to your partner to be as sensitive as possible. It's never easy to finish with someone because you know that at best the person will be feeling hurt, and at worst he or she will be devastated. Either way, you'll be feeling pretty guilty.

You've got to be responsible and think of your ex-partner's feelings. It's cruel to walk away without an explanation – you wouldn't like someone to treat you that way. It takes courage, but the honest way to make a clean break is to say something like, "Look, I really don't think this is working for us, at least not for me. How do you feel?" (See below.)

Try to remain friends with your ex-partner so that he or she doesn't become excluded from groups of mutual friends, as this causes lasting resentment. By acting maturely, you can make it much easier for both of you to get over the breakup.

DO'S & DON'TS

BE TACTFUL
Do tell your partner first.

BE DISCREET
Don't be unkind about your ex-partner to other people.

AVOID HUMILIATION
Don't snub your ex-partner by suddenly appearing with a replacement (see below).

STAY IN TOUCH
Do offer to remain friends.

NEXT TIME . . .

If you're ending a relationship or feeling rejected, think about any mistakes you made and try to learn from them. To help put things into perspective, read your Bill of Rights on page 34.

BREAKING IT OFF WITH SOMEONE

At least I know where I stand now.

Hope he doesn't hate me!

But I thought we were an item!

Ha! That got rid of him.

✓ "Look, I'm really sorry, but it's just not working out."

✗ "Get lost, John. I'm going out with someone else tonight."

. . . at LEAST one brush-off.

WHAT COULD

Sexual

HAPPEN NEXT

health and pregnancy

Sex can have some unwanted fallout if you're not careful. Some of the infections that you can contract through sex are incurable, such as herpes, or even fatal, such as AIDS. So take care. Remember, contraceptives can prevent pregnancy, and condoms in particular can prevent STDs from being passed on. One hasty action can ruin your whole life, so never take a chance. If you do get into trouble, don't keep your problems to yourself. Get advice and treatment immediately. There are some things that no one should try to cope with alone.

Why oh why didn't we use protection? It would have been so easy to have prevented this.

NO CURE FOR HIV

AIDS ALERT

COPING WITH STDs

STD stands for "*sexually* transmitted disease"

These infections are *only* spread during SEX

If you're not CAREFUL, you could spread an STD

WHAT IS AN STD?

The labels "sexually transmitted disease" (STD) and "venereal disease" (VD) both mean the same thing – diseases that have been passed on during sexual intercourse. There are several different STDs, most of which are treatable.

THE MAIN STDs

- **Genital warts, nonspecific urethritis (NSU), herpes**
  Viral infections, mostly incurable, but symptoms can be treated.
- **Gonorrhea, syphilis, chlamydia**
  Bacterial infections, treatable with antibiotics.
- **HIV/AIDS, hepatitis B**
  Incurable, fatal viral infections (see page 72).
- **Lice, scabies**
  Parasites, treated with insecticides.
- **Monilia, candida**
  Yeasts treated with fungicide.
- **Trichomonas**
  Single cell parasite, treatable with antibiotics.

GETTING HELP

Hope I don't sound too nervous.

"Oh, ummm, h-h-hello. Could you tell me what time the clinic's open, please?"

This one sounds like he could use a little reassurance.

"Every weekday between nine and six. Feel free to drop in anytime."

REMEMBER... The only sure way ....

WHAT TO DO

If ever you suspect that you may have an STD, or that you have been in contact with someone who has one, see your doctor or visit your local special clinic at once. Get the address from information in the phone book (see page 92). Treatment at the clinic is free and confidential, but you will be asked for a list of contacts that you have had some form of sex with.

SUSPECT SYMPTOMS

Seek medical help immediately if you have any of these symptoms:
- Pain when you urinate.
- Heavy, discolored discharge that doesn't smell right.
- Discharge that gives you a rash or makes you sore or itchy.
- Lower back pain, or pain in the front of the pelvis, or groin.
- Pain when having sex.
- Sore spots on the genital area.
If you've had anal sex, watch for symptoms around the anus; if you've had oral sex, watch for symptoms around the mouth.

IF YOU BECOME INFECTED

STOP SEX
Give up sex immediately.

TELL YOUR PARTNER
It's difficult, but you must tell your partner or partners, past and present. If they don't know, they may reinfect you and others.

FIND THE SOURCE
Ask your partner or partners to track down the people that they may have had sexual contact with.

NEXT TIME . . .

Never have unprotected sex, even with someone you know. Insist that your partner has only one sexual partner and that's you.

"Next patient, number six! Please follow me."

"You have to go or we'll both get it again. Don't worry, they're okay there."

. . to avoid STDs is not to have sex.

THE TRUTH ABOUT HIV

HIV is usually *transmitted* through SEXUAL activity

It's *hard* to catch HIV, but if you do, it's INCURABLE

AIDS is the *terminal* stage of HIV infection

When you are armed with the facts about HIV (Human Immuno-deficiency Virus) and willing to take some sensible precautions, you can protect yourself against infection and still enjoy sex. Infection with the HIV virus leads eventually to AIDS (Acquired Immune Deficiency Syndrome), which causes the body to lose its ability to fight a variety of fatal infections and cancers. HIV is the most dangerous of all STDs (sexually transmitted diseases), because at the moment, there are no vaccines or cures. Although treatments have been developed that slow down the effects of the virus, it is still fatal.

FACTS ABOUT HIV AND AIDS

● It takes 3–6 months for the virus to be detectable in the body.
● The HIV test becomes positive because you have developed antibodies to the virus. The detection of antibodies is just a way of showing you have the virus.
● It can take 10 years or more for an HIV-positive person to develop full-blown AIDS.
● AIDS-related diseases include fatal pneumonia, skin cancer (Kaposi's sarcoma), and dementia (deterioration of the brain).

PROTECT YOURSELF

● Avoid any sex with transmission of semen, blood and vaginal fluid between you and another person – even oral sex is risky.
● Never have unprotected sex. Wearing a condom greatly reduces the risk of contracting HIV.
● Intravenous drug-users should never share equipment.
● If you decide to get a tattoo or have your body pierced, make sure it's done by a reputable person.

GETTING HELP. . .

Anyone contemplating having an HIV test should also have counseling, available at all STD clinics. Always exercise your right to talk to a counselor. There are many support groups that not only help people who have contracted HIV infection or developed AIDS, but also their families and their close friends (see page 92).

NEXT TIME . . .

There is no next time with AIDS. Seek counseling immediately if you are at all worried. This is a condition that no one should face alone.

REMEMBER... Unprotected sex is like a . . .

WE'RE ALL AT RISK WITH HIV

HIV isn't an infection that picks on certain types of people. Both men and women are at risk, and straight people can be just as vulnerable as gay men. The diagram below shows the most common routes of infection. Getting HIV has nothing to do with who you are – but it has a lot to do with what you do. You owe it to yourself and your partner not to be complacent.

Sex with a homosexual man	*Sharing needles for drugs*	*Sex with a bisexual man*	*Infected blood*

Likely routes of infection

Sex with an infected person
The most common route of infection is sexual intercourse; semen or, more rarely, vaginal fluids can contain enough of the virus to give you the disease.

High-risk sex
Anal intercourse is particularly risky when unprotected. If the anal passage gets bruised and torn, the virus can gain rapid entry via the partner's semen.

Sharing needles for drugs
Intravenous drug users who are HIV-positive and share needles and other paraphernalia, pass the virus on through their blood-contaminated equipment.

Infected blood
At one time people became infected with HIV through contaminated blood transfusions or blood products, but this risk has been greatly reduced.

. . game of Russian ROULETTE.

THE TRUTH ABOUT HIV *continued*

NEVER HAVE SEX WITH A STRANGER

No matter how much you like someone, never give in to the temptation of having sex with a partner you barely know. Talk to him or her before you do anything you might regret (see right). Talk about the risk; if he or she gets angry or resentful, you should ask yourself whether this person is really worth knowing.

Because boys are just as worried about AIDS as girls are, they're usually grateful if the girl raises the subject, as long as it's done in a tactful way.

I really like him but we've only just met. Mustn't do anything stupid.

"Oh come on, what harm can it do? I really want you Sarah."

ONCE IS ENOUGH

AIDS was first identified in homosexual men, and for some years, few women became infected. Women who do not have sex with men, receive transfusions, or share needles are unlikely to catch HIV.

But many tragic cases of AIDS among single and married women and men have borne out the theory that just one sexual contact with an infected person is enough for someone to contract HIV.

PREGNANCY AND HIV/AIDS

A woman who is infected with HIV when she becomes pregnant can pass the infection on to her baby, either while the baby is in her womb, or during the birth. But not all babies remain HIV-positive; if the antibodies (see page 72) in the baby's blood come from the mother, having passed across the placenta, they may disappear after about 18 months. However, infected mothers are still advised not to breastfeed, as the virus can be passed to the baby in breast milk.

THE HIDDEN VIRUS

All people who have contracted the virus (whether they are HIV-positive or not), can pass the virus on to others, even if they appear healthy and free of symptoms. A person does not have to be ill with AIDS to infect others. This is why it's so important to use a condom.

WARNING . . .

The only sure way to avoid HIV infection is not to have unprotected sex. It can make sexual relationships more difficult – but the risk is too great to compromise.

REMEMBER . . . There is NO second chance .

MYTHS ABOUT HIV INFECTION

Because HIV/AIDS is a very frightening subject, a lot of myths and half-truths have sprung up about how these infections can be transmitted. But it should be stressed that HIV is a virus that is difficult to catch. The virus is found only in blood, semen, and vaginal fluids, usually in fairly small numbers. Knowing the truth about HIV helps you to act responsibly.

● YOU WON'T GET HIV from swimming in the same pool as an HIV-positive person.

● YOU WON'T GET HIV if you kiss an infected person on the mouth, though there is a slight risk if the person has inflamed or bleeding gums.

There ought to be separate toilets for those HIV people.

I hope they wash the glasses well in this place.

● YOU WON'T GET HIV sitting on a toilet seat that's been used by an infected person.

● YOU WON'T GET HIV if someone sneezes; the virus doesn't travel through the air.

● YOU WON'T GET HIV by drinking from a glass or eating from a plate that's been used by an HIV-positive person.

● YOU WON'T GET HIV by going to school or college with an HIV-positive person; visiting someone with HIV at their home or in the hospital; hugging, shaking hands, or dancing with someone who is HIV-positive.

That's it! I'm done for. I've heard you can catch AIDS from a mosquito bite.

● YOU WON'T GET HIV if you're bitten by an insect. Or if you donate blood at a blood bank, donor clinic, or hospital.

. . . with AIDS.

GETTING PREGNANT

SEX can lead to pregnancy even with *contraception*

If you think you're **PREGNANT**, don't keep it *secret*

TELL your *parents* as soon as possible

FIRST REACTIONS

Fear and disbelief are common reactions when you discover that you're pregnant, but however scared you feel, you should never keep your pregnancy a secret. Confide in your parents or your doctor at once.

TELLING YOUR PARENTS

● If you find it easier to talk to your mother, tell her first, and ask her to tell her dad (see opposite).
● It can help if you tell a close relative – someone your parents trust – and take this person along.
● Consider your options before talking to your parents; let them see how responsible you can be.

An unwanted pregnancy is difficult for everyone concerned. Most unexpected pregnancies occur through ignorance or mistakes, but you can get pregnant even when you use contraception (see pages 62–3). If you're pregnant, it's too late for regrets. Take positive action.

GIRLS: TELLING YOUR PARTNER

If the father wants to be involved but disagrees about the course of action, listen, but explain that the final decision is yours. If he won't support you, try to get by without him for now; you have enough to worry about.

BOYS: GETTING THE NEWS

Try to remember that while you are equally responsible, your girlfriend's burden is infinitely greater than yours. Ultimately you cannot control events, but you'll never have a better opportunity to give your partner your full support.

REMEMBER . . . For the sake of your health . .

HOW TO TELL IF YOU'RE PREGNANT

If you have any of the symptoms below, go straight to your doctor or family planning clinic and ask for a pregnancy test. You'll need to take along a small sample of your urine. For quick results, home pregnancy kits can be bought from any drugstore.

- A missed period, if your periods are regular.
- A short scanty period at the correct time.
- Swollen tingling breasts and darkening nipples.
- Wanting to pass urine more often than usual.

- More vaginal discharge than you usually have.
- Feeling really tired.
- A strange taste in your mouth.
- Disliking food you liked before.
- Feeling sick, particularly if you go without food, such as early in the morning.

BREAKING THE NEWS

Don't change color. Don't let me be pregnant.

"According to this I'm pregnant. This can't be happening to me."

Robbie's being so supportive. I'm glad I told him right away.

"Don't you think it would be best to tell your mother, Alison?"

Now that mom knows, everything's going to be okay.

"Now, now, don't worry. I'll tell dad and we'll go and see the doctor."

He's taking it well. It's good to know that Alison really trusts us.

"Well, I can't pretend it isn't a shock. But I'm just relieved she told us."

. . get HELP quickly.

GETTING PREGNANT *continued*

GETTING HELP

Once you have confirmed the pregnancy, you need to consider the options that are open to you. Although you should talk to your parents and partner, you must also seek professional help. You can talk to your doctor in confidence, and he or she may refer you to a therapist or counselor. There are also some specialized clinics that you can contact. If you decide to have the baby, you'll need good prenatal care, so the sooner your pregnancy is being guided by a doctor, the better.

If you want to put the baby up for adoption, you can get confidential advice from special adoption agencies or social-service departments. See page 92 for some useful addresses and hotlines.

IF YOU'RE STILL AT SCHOOL

If you have not completed your education but decide to have the baby, you need to consider your options carefully.

● Are you above or below the legal age for compulsory schooling? Your guidance counselor can advise you on how to continue your education throughout your pregnancy and after the birth.

● You may feel tempted to leave school right away, but try to think of your long-term future before making any rash decisions. You still need education for your career and your self-esteem.

IF YOU'RE A FATHER

If your girlfriend is pregnant, you will certainly have opinions about what your partner should do. In most states you have no legal right to a say in whether she goes ahead with the pregnancy or not. However, this doesn't mean you should be excluded from discussions. Your attitude and support will count for a lot in helping your partner to make up her mind. Fathers have rights once the baby is born, and with those rights come all the many responsibilities of having a family.

I don't know who's more obsessed with this baby – me or my mom and dad.

It's wonderful having a baby in the house again!

Doting grandparents
Many parents may enjoy sharing in the care of their new grandchild. Others don't.

REMEMBER... Bringing up a child . . . .

IT'S YOUR DECISION

You may receive a lot of well-meaning advice on what to do about your pregnancy. You may even feel pressured into doing something that someone else thinks is "right," but in the end it is your decision.

I have found that attitudes among teenage mothers vary so widely that it would be impossible – and highly inappropriate – to recommend any particular course of action for pregnant teenagers. While some girls are convinced that the best thing for the baby is to have it adopted, others cannot bear the idea of giving their child away. For those who find the idea of teenage motherhood unacceptable, the only answer is to have an abortion.

The right choice for you

In addition to your partner, parents, and a close relative, try always to confide in a doctor, or a member of the clergy if you have a religious background. But in the end, whatever anyone else says, you have to weigh your future, your strengths, your weaknesses, your ambitions, and the strength of your maternal drive. Only you know how you want your life to be, so only you can make the right decision.

WARNING . . .

Don't allow yourself to be forced into a decision that you're unhappy with because it seems to be the easiest. You will always regret it.

SOME OF YOUR OPTIONS

GET MARRIED
Get married to the father and have the baby.

LIVE TOGETHER
Live with the father and raise the child together.

BE A SINGLE MOTHER
Bring up the child on your own as a single parent.

START OVER
Sometimes an abortion is the only answer (see page 80).

FAMILY AFFAIR
Have the baby and stay with your parents (see opposite), who may be willing to help you care for the child.

ANOTHER HOME
Get the baby adopted by a loving family.

Adoption
It's a relief to know your baby will be well cared for.

. . . is a LIFELONG commitment.

ENDING A PREGNANCY

Abortion is **NEVER** an *easy* decision

There's *always* going to be **EMOTIONAL** suffering

Abortion is **NOT** a form of *birth control*

I'm so relieved she told me about it.

I'm glad I told mom, I don't feel so alone now.

A DIFFICULT DECISION

If you have weighed all the choices that are open to you (see pages 78–9), and decided to end your pregnancy, then you should see your doctor as soon as you can about obtaining an abortion.

Different countries have different legal criteria and restrictions regarding abortion, but no doctor likes to perform an abortion after 12 weeks. You should *never* contemplate seeking an illegal abortion, or try to abort the fetus yourself – *you could die*. At the very least, the damage could prevent you from being able to have children in the future.

WHAT IS ABORTION?

An abortion (termination) is the medical procedure that ends a pregnancy by removing the fetus from the womb. If you are pregnant and feel that this is the only way out, you should talk to your doctor as soon as possible.

GETTING COUNSELING

I feel so guilty and depressed. Why is this happening to me?

She needs an expert to comfort her.

She really understands how I feel.

In time she'll see that she made the right decision for her circumstances.

"Come on honey, the counselor will be able to put your mind at ease."

"It's natural to feel like this, Kim, and you don't have to go through it alone."

REMEMBER... Most abortions . . . .

THINK ABOUT...

● It's important to plan ahead, because an abortion is rarely performed in less than a week from first seeing a doctor, and it may be a few weeks. It is safer and less traumatic emotionally to have an abortion sooner, rather than later.

● Be prepared to experience some confusing feelings, before and after the abortion. Before, you'll think about the baby growing inside you and be wracked with guilt, but afterward you may feel relieved because you were really not ready to bring a child into the world.

● Even though you may be terrified of discussing the idea of abortion with your parents, try to take them into your confidence. Loving parents will ensure that you get the right kind of help, and their support will ease some of the anxiety that you're going through.

● If you feel that you cannot talk to your parents or family doctor, go to an independent organization that specializes in giving advice about unplanned pregnancies (see page 92 for some helpful addresses and telephone numbers).

COPING WITH YOUR FEELINGS

After an abortion it's common to feel withdrawn, tearful, and unable to make decisions. But take heart; along with the sadness will come a sense of relief.

If your depression persists, see your doctor. Most abortion clinics have a counselor you can confide in, and some professional support can really help you start feeling better about yourself (see opposite).

DO'S AND DON'TS AFTER ABORTION

TAKE IT EASY
Do look after yourself by resting for at least a day.

NO EXERCISE
Don't get any strenuous exercise for at least three days.

TAMPONS AND PADS
Don't use any tampons for two or three weeks to avoid the risk of infection; sanitary napkins are fine.

CHECKUP
Do have a medical checkup within a week of the abortion, even if you feel fine.

SYMPTOMS
Do consult your doctor immediately if you start to vomit or bleed heavily, or if you have prolonged vaginal discharge or a fever.

BIRTH CONTROL
Do use reliable birth control immediately; you don't want to get pregnant again.

NEXT TIME . . .

Abortion is a tragedy, so make sure there isn't going to be a "next time". Get information on contraception now (see pages 62–3). Think of the results of all of your actions.

. . . are AVOIDABLE.

EXPLORATION

Masturbation, and Being Gay

Many people get to know themselves sexually through the safe and private exploration of masturbation. This is perfectly healthy! Fantasies are natural as well; everyone has them. As long as you don't hurt anyone, you should never feel guilty. In addition, no matter what anyone says, you have as much right to be homosexual as heterosexual.

As a younger person, you may need support and courage to begin with in order to live the life you want without interference from other people.

GOING IT ALONE

Almost *everyone* has sexual **FANTASIES** now and then

Masturbation is a **NORMAL** sexual *expression*

There's no **NEED** to feel *guilty* about either

MASTURBATION

Touching yourself "down below" is a perfectly normal habit no matter what age, gender, or sexual orientation you happen to be. Masturbation is not wrong and it never does any harm, unless it turns into an obsessive occupation. It may indicate deeper problems that have to do with poor self-esteem.

Although it's common for boys to masturbate more frequently than girls, masturbation is more important to girls because it allows them to explore and experiment with their bodies long before they have sex with another person.

Although they may not often admit it, a lot of boys and girls achieve their best orgasms by masturbating. Nowadays, I am pleased to say, the majority of young people believe that it is acceptable and harmless to do this, and of course they are right.

WORRIES AND QUESTIONS. . .

Masturbation will not make you go blind! Nor will it give you bad skin, insanity, or hairy palms – these are all myths. It is also quite normal to fantasize about somebody while you are masturbating, and these fantasies are almost always innocent. Most people have no difficulty in drawing the line between fantasy and reality, and do not want to act out their fantasies.

Undesirable influences
In recent years people have begun to worry about the possibility of young people, and even children, being influenced by unnecessarily extreme sexual images in movies, magazines, and on the Internet. Don't just dismiss this unease as an overreaction; nobody questions the idea that images of an uplifting nature in art and books are "good" influences – so why shouldn't the opposite be true?

Don't ever allow yourself to be influenced by images of sex-related violence on women and children, which cater to certain warped fantasies, or you'll be playing straight into the hands of the people who exploit these harmful images for profit.

REMEMBER . . . Masturbation NEVER did . . .

EXPLORING YOUR FANTASIES

As you become more sexually aware, it's perfectly normal to start fantasizing about sex. Many people fantasize during masturbation and even sexual intercourse.

● The most common fantasy for boys and men is imagining the nude body of a girl or woman; boys can be sexually aroused simply by seeing pictures of nudity.

● Girls' fantasies are much more specific and rarely anonymous. Most girls fantasize about a particular boyfriend, or a hero who turns them on.

● Girls who have not yet had a full sexual relationship tend to have simple fantasies about being kissed on a first date, or a boyfriend saying "I love you."

GETTING HELP

If you're a girl and you've never experienced an orgasm, masturbation can be useful for exploring how your clitoris should be stimulated. Try it and see what happens!

Fantasy and your partner
Both boys and girls may fantasize about their partners when they masturbate, but for girls this is more important.

. . anyone any harm.

BEING GAY

There's *nothing wrong* with being **HOMOSEXUAL**

Same-sex **RELATIONSHIPS** can be lasting

There's *no need* to **HIDE** your preference

FACTS ABOUT HOMOSEXUALITY

Every person should have the right to choose who and how they love, and this includes homosexual love. Being homosexual means being attracted to and preferring sex with someone of the same gender. Nowadays people who prefer someone of their own gender are often referred to as being "gay," although this is more often applied to male homosexuals. Female homosexuals are called lesbians; lesbian relationships are those in which women share joy and sexual fulfillment with other women. In the past homosexuality was viewed as abnormal, but we now know this attitude to be wrong; most people accept that homosexuals have the same rights as anyone.

ATTRACTION TO THE SAME SEX

While many teenagers have a sexual experience with someone of the same sex when they're young, this doesn't mean that they're homosexual. In your early teens, you may have had a homosexual "crush" on an older pupil, a teacher at school, an actor, or a famous musician.

There's nothing unusual or abnormal about having a crush. Crushes are a natural part of your awakening sexual awareness and, as long as you don't go and do anything silly, crushes serve a useful purpose because they help you to start to understand what love is really like.

BEING AROUSED

A boy may get an erection if he feels love, excitement, or attraction for another boy. This sometimes happens when boys "horse around" in mock fights and wrestling, and it's a normal part of growing up; it doesn't necessarily mean you're gay – although you may be. Girls also feel attraction for other girls, especially older girls. And again, this is a normal part of their sexual awakening.

REMEMBER...Love is the same, whether . . .

FINDING LOVE

"Joe, Kim, sorry I'm late! Oh, hello, who's your friend?"

"Whoa! If you're trying to drown me, you're doing a good job!"

"I'm having a really fantastic day! It's been great meeting you."

"John and Peter seem to be getting along very well, don't you think?"

ARE GAY PEOPLE THAT DIFFERENT?

COMPANIONSHIP
Just like everyone else, gay people value long-term friendship and closeness, and respect each other's feelings.

SEX LIFE
Sexual activities aren't that different from non-gays; gay people kiss and stimulate each other in the usual ways. Some male gays agree to have anal sex, but then so do some straight couples.

STAYING TOGETHER
Many gay partnerships outlast conventional marriages.

COMING TO TERMS WITH YOUR SEXUALITY

If you find that you continue to feel attracted to people of your own sex as you get older, you may decide that you want to live a gay lifestyle. According to most gay men and lesbians, you will instinctively know that this is right for you. But there's an obvious problem – how are you going to meet like-minded people?

Without help, you're going to feel really isolated, so try phoning a gay or lesbian support service, or joining a gay or lesbian group. Many newspapers carry addresses and telephone numbers of local lesbian and gay organizations. See page 92 for some useful addresses and hotlines.

. . it's heterosexual or homosexual.

BEING GAY *continued*

WORRIES AND QUESTIONS. . .

Even though gay people are more widely accepted in society than they used to be, and even though they have the same legal rights as heterosexuals, prejudice still exists. Because of this, many young gays are afraid to admit that they're homosexual, especially to their parents, and try to live a lie. Even in the quite recent past, some gay people have even covered up by getting married and having a family before gaining the courage to "come out" in their thirties or forties.

If you are gay, it's important that you try to find the self-confidence to be open about your sexual preferences. Your own friends of both sexes will probably be the first to come forward in supporting you. Your family may take some time to get used to the idea, but they may be a lot more open-minded than you think.

UNSYMPATHETIC FAMILIES

There's no way around it – some parents are going to freak out when they learn that you are gay. They probably don't mean to be cruel, but their behavior will make you feel isolated and alone. Seek help and advice from a local gay or lesbian hotline (see page 92 for useful numbers). There are many other gay people in your situation, and they may be able to offer some coping strategies.

GAYS AT SCHOOL

Some teenagers know deep down inside that they are gay from an early age. If boys and girls at school suspect that another pupil is gay, they can be painfully cruel. No one should be made to feel inferior by their peers, and if the situation gets out of control, you should confide in a sympathetic friend or a member of staff.

MEETING THE PARENTS

"Don't worry about tonight. My parents are really cool about meeting you."

"Well, this is a nice evening! You and Paul must visit us soon."

REMEMBER... Be PROUD of yourself . . .

LESBIAN LOVERS

We hear an awful lot about male homosexuality but less about female homosexuality (known as lesbianism), although the two groups have much in common. Lesbianism is as natural, though not as common, as heterosexuality. Lesbians are not biologically different from other women, nor do they have (as some people would have you believe), different family backgrounds from heterosexual women. While most women opt for heterosexuality, some accept a heterosexual lifestyle while continuing to have important and loving relationships with women. Others choose a completely lesbian lifestyle.

Being positive

Many lesbians look back over their childhood searching for early symptoms or causes of lesbianism, such as having lesbian dreams, or crushes on older girls, or female teachers. But there's no need to try to rationalize things in this way. Being a lesbian is simply about how you want to live your life.

In fact, lesbianism is sometimes more a choice of lifestyle than a sexual choice. Lesbian relationships are often based less on sex than heterosexual relationships. They may have more to do with a desire to relate to other women.

Sex between women is of the same nature as sex between men and women. It's just as intense, passionate, loving, warm, and caring. But just like heterosexual love, it can also prove to be disappointing and destructive.

MYTHS ABOUT LESBIANS

SUPER SEXY
Lesbians aren't sexual superwomen; they are no more or less sexually active than heterosexual women.

EQUALITY RULES!
The idea that one woman plays the part of the "man," and the other plays the part of the "woman" is a myth.

MAN HATERS
Lesbians don't hate men, just as gay men don't hate women. Gay people have friends of both sexes.

NEXT TIME . . .
Think about: If you're not gay, but you know someone who is, don't give them a hard time for their choice of lifestyle. Homosexual love is as valid as heterosexual love.

. . whatever your sexual IDENTITY.

LOOKING AHEAD

Throughout this book I've tried to stress that your sexual responsibilities need to be approached thoughtfully, because the way that you handle your relationships can have a significant bearing on how you relate to the rest of the world.

Adults who still have their own unresolved hang-ups and irrational fears about sex are usually horrified when they learn that young people are sexually active, and their knee-jerk response is to attempt a ban. But you should have the right to make your own decisions. Everyone has the right to live a healthy sexual life, and that involves seeking some basic freedoms, though not all adults will agree with my list.

● **Freedom from sexual stereotyping**
Don't buy into the idea that men should be aggressive, strong, and dominant, and that women should be passive, weak, emotional, and submissive. These old-fashioned stereotypes have no place in an honest relationship. The best relationships give each partner an equal chance to be themselves.

● **Freedom from sexual oppression**
Be aware of sexual exploitation – in our society women are often reduced to sexual objects and exploited as workers. They also receive little recognition for being housewives and mothers. Before any two people can relate with sexual honesty, they have to be aware of these inequalities and try to resist them.

● **Freedom of information**
Suitable basic information about sex should be available to everyone, regardless of age, sex, or intelligence.

● **Freedom from repression by the older generation**
Many parents do not have adequate information about sexual behavior or, if they do, are unable or unwilling to share it. Many find it difficult just coming to terms with their child's emerging sexuality.

● **Freedom to control one's own body**
This would question laws that restrict medical abortions, voluntary sterilization, consenting sexual relations among adults, and contraceptive information and practical help for young people.

● **Freedom of sexual expression for disabled people**
People with learning difficulties, mental illness, or physical disabilities still have the right to sexual expression, and special efforts should be made to help them find appropriate sexual opportunities.

THINK ABOUT . . .
As you become more mature, you have clearer perceptions of what you want out of life, and what you can put into it. If you can bring a degree of mature thought to your sexual relationships, and also share your thoughts with your partner, you will ultimately achieve a generous sexual relationship that is life-enhancing and of which you can both be proud.

USEFUL ADDRESSES

SEXUALITY

SIECUS (The Sexuality Information and Education Council of the US)
130 West 42nd Street,
Suite 350
New York, NY 10036
Tel: (212) 819-9770

Provides information about all facets of sexuality.

Teen Council
1025 Vermont Ave. NW, Suite 200
Washington, DC 20005
Tel: (202) 347-5700

Answers questions about sexuality, STD prevention, birth control, and related issues.

PREGNANCY & CONTRACEPTION

The Door
555 Broome St.
New York, NY 10013
Tel: (212) 941-9090

Offers sexual awareness programs and counseling to the youth of New York; write for literature.

MELD for Young Moms
123 N. Third Street, Suite 507
Minneapolis, MN 55401
Tel: (612) 332-7563

Education and support groups for teenage mothers.

National Adoption Counseling Service
Tel: (800) 341-5959

Counseling and referrals to state adoption agencies.

The National Abortion and Reproductive Rights Action League
1156 15th Street NW, Suite 700
Washington, DC 20005
Tel: (202) 973-3000

An activist organization that seeks to protect reproductive freedom.

National Abortion Federation Hotline
Tel: (800) 772-9100

Provides advice about abortion and pregnancy, reproductive laws, and offers information about the facilities available to women.

Planned Parenthood, Inc.
810 Seventh Ave.
New York, NY 10019
Tel: (800) 829-7732
Tel: (800) 230-7526

Offers birth control services, pregnancy tests, prenatal care, STD education and treatment, AIDS testing, and HIV counseling.

SUPPORT FOR GAYS & LESBIANS

The Gay and Lesbian Anti-Violence Project
Tel: (212) 807-0197

Crisis intervention for gay, lesbian, and bisexual people who have been verbally or physically assaulted.

The Gay and Lesbian National Hotline
Tel: (888) 843-4564

Counseling and information for gays, lesbians, and bisexuals, and those struggling with sexual orientation.

HIV/AIDS & OTHER SEXUALLY TRANSMITTED DISEASES

AIDS Hotline (US Department of Health and Human Services)
Tel: (800) 342-AIDS

General information about AIDS and HIV; referrals provided.

AIDS Treatment Information Service
Tel: (800) HIV-0440

Information on treating HIV; referrals available.

Herpes Resource Center
Tel: (800) 230-6039

Information on the prevention and treatment of herpes.

The Multicultural AIDS Coalition
Douglas Park
801-B Tremont Street
Boston, MA 02118
Tel: (617) 442-1622

Information about HIV and AIDS that addresses people of color.

National Sexually Transmitted Disease Hotline
Tel: (800) 227-8922

Answers to questions about STDs, and referrals to local clinics.

Project Inform Treatment Hotline
Tel: (800) 822-7422

Information and referral for HIV-infected individuals.

Safe Choice Hotline
Tel: (800) 878-2437

Counseling and information for teenagers, especially about pregnancy and STD prevention.

ADVICE & COUNSELING

American Self-Help Clearing House
Tel: (212) 625-7105

Provides nationwide listings of support groups for young people who are facing various issues and concerns.

Covenant House Nineline
Tel: (800) 999-9999

Crisis intervention for all teenagers, particularly runaways and homeless youth.

Family Resources Warm Line
Tel: (800) 641-4546

Provides nonmedical parenting advice, support, and referrals.

The National Child Abuse Hotline
Tel: (800) 422-4453

Help for victims of past or present child abuse.

NEDO (The National Eating Disorders Organization)
62655 South Yale Street
Tulsa, OK 74136
Tel: (918) 481-4044

Advice, information, and counseling on eating disorders.

RAINN (Rape, Abuse, Incest National Network)
Tel: (800) 656-HOPE

For victims of any kind of sexual assault; call this number to be automatically connected to a rape crisis center in your area.

INDEX

ACKNOWLEDGMENTS

Dorling Kindersley would like to thank: Gary Ombler for photography; Adam Moore for DTP work; Glenda Fisher for design assistance; Daisy Hayden and Rob Watson for research; Hilary Bird for the index.